NY Votes for Women:
A Suffrage Centennial Anthology

NY Votes for Women: A Suffrage Centennial Anthology

Stacey Murphy and Nora Snyder, Editors

Cayuga Lake Books
Ithaca, NY

Cayuga Lake Books
Ithaca, New York USA

cayugalakebooks.com

NY Votes for Women: A Suffrage Centennial Anthology
edited by Stacey Murphy and Nora Snyder

First Printing – October 2017
ISBN: 978-1-68111-199-5
Library of Congress Control Number: 2017952812

Front cover image: Trixie Friganza between suffrage leaders [New York], c. 1908 by the Bain News Service. Courtesy of the Library of Congress, LC-DIG-ggbain-02466

Back cover image: January 2017 photograph of the Women's March in Ithaca, New York
Photo credit: Alison Fromme

Cover design by St. John Design Group

Printed in the U.S.A.

The initial printing of this book was made possible by with funding from the Community Arts Partnership of Tompkins County.

COMMUNITY
ARTS
PARTNERSHIP

Printed in the U.S.A.

CONTENTS

INTRODUCTIONS

I've long enjoyed history, especially learning about the things that weren't taught in classes or history books. Everything that has ever happened to people, when placed against the backdrop of the times they lived in, becomes social history—and when told well, who doesn't love a good story? Stories in context help us sift through the details of our own lives and decide what meanings to give them. Which details are significant? Which are minor? How do they signify in the broader world?

There are many more stories we don't know than we do. History lessons that were drilled into our consciousness in school have been wanting for feminine leaders and perspectives to balance those of men. Foremothers did great things, too.

I've heard some fascinating anecdotes during this project. One friend who is researching the Statue of Liberty told me that American women were not allowed on Liberty Island during the October 1886 unveiling, though two French women, Jeanne-Emile Bartholdi, wife of the statue's designer, and the 13-year-old daughter of Ferdinand de Lesseps, a French engineer who spoke that day, were permitted to attend the ceremony. Women suffragists from New York chartered a boat which circled the island, shouting speeches in protest that they didn't have liberty to vote even though Lady Liberty was meant to embody the spirit of the American dream for all.

Why have we not heard more stories like this? Another writer friend told a story about growing up in the same Western Pennsylvania town where Ida Tarbell had lived. She remembers the historic marker in front of the house, but no one ever told her much of Ida's story. Tarbell had been the journalist—"a muckraker," she was called—who exposed John D. Rockefeller's ruthless practices in the oil industry, and her articles led to the Supreme Court's breakup of the Standard Oil monopoly. It seemed that there wasn't any sentiment against Tarbell, but no one found her relevant in the course of considering the other matters of their daily lives in that little town.

All of our history and herstory deserve the chance to matter. There is much at stake for women in 2017: basic health care, reproductive rights, violence control, and workers' rights including pay equality. In addition, threatened elimination of Federal programs for the Arts and the Humanities signifies the current administration's disdain for telling the stories of our history about, and to, the common man and woman. *NY Votes for Women: A Suffrage Centennial Anthology*, in that context, has felt all the more important to complete now.

As we've been gathering stories, it's become clear that the suffragists' struggles of 100+ years ago resonate for many people who draw parallels between that history and more recent battles to gain or keep our rights. As we are becoming more aware that the way forward needs an intersectional[1] approach, those voices bring a modern, more inclusive lens to the ways in which we relate to the past. We sought out a diverse set of voices and viewpoints, including some not heard during the original suffrage movement. The stories and writings in this anthology represent a variety of times, locations, and viewpoints over the last century in New York State. They include non-white and immigrant voices. They include voices of suffragists in the 1900s to those of the 2017 Women's March participants.

Here's to our voices and our stories!

- Stacey Murphy

---

[1] *Intersectionality is a term coined by American civil rights advocate Kimberlé Williams Crenshaw to describe overlapping or intersecting social identities and related systems of oppression, domination, or discrimination.*

Partnering with Stacey Murphy on the Women's Suffrage Centennial Anthology project has been an honor, a pleasure, and an exciting opportunity to bring forth a work that is needed and desired in the world right now.

The project was a natural extension of the issues and concepts we had visited during our meetings of Writer's Block Party, a group I created to gather local writers in "real life" and online space, where we discussed things like voice, vulnerability, and mission in connection with our writing. Our meeting discussions and this project both reflected the greater political realities and social landscape of our times. They also tapped into an internal hunger from writers to be heard, sharing stories and impressions that they may not otherwise have had the impetus or forum for. The Women's Suffrage Centennial Anthology became a container for all of it—the memories, the feelings, the frustrations, the truths. The Anthology emerged with passion and urgency as a statement and record of our times.

It wasn't all easy. The history associated with the Women's Suffrage Movement is in some ways shadowy and elusive because many of us have very little exposure to events not emphasized in our history books. As writers and women, we had to navigate questions like, "How do we reference the suffrage movement in a way that feels authentic to us?" and "Is this a story we individually belong in given our diversity in ages, ethnicities, races, and gender identities?" These hard questions resonated deeply, beyond our anthology microcosm, as we strove for enlightened inclusivity and intersectionality in our society today.

I believe Writer's Block Party provided a safe space in which to wade through our "blocks" of discomfort and fear and lack of clarity, serving as a support group and an experimental writing lab to fortify our contributors and drive the anthology to fruition. I feel blessed to have had the task of lovingly collecting and honing the eclectic contributions of our writers with their many fascinating angles and tangents relating to women and the vote. One of the many gifts of this project has been finding ourselves vulnerable yet stronger through these stories, with all our differences and varied perspectives, as we share and build and co-create our own herstory.

Welcome to the Anthology! We hope you enjoy it.

- Nora Snyder

CAROL KAMMEN, TOMPKINS COUNTY HISTORIAN
Foreword – 2017: Year of the Woman

On January 3, 2017, in recognition of the centennial of the passage of the Suffrage Act in New York in the year 1917, the Tompkins County Legislature passed a proclamation declaring 2017 the Year of the Woman in Tompkins County.

The proclamation recognizes the long struggle for a woman to be able to take her place as an equal citizen in the world outside her home.

The issue of a woman's place in the world was recognized by Abigail Adams, in her 1776 letter to her husband John, then attending the Continental Congress in Philadelphia. She broached the issue of suffrage, urging him "to remember the ladies." She stated her desire that he "would be more generous and favorable to them than your ancestors. Do not put such unlimited power in the hands of the husbands. Remember, all men would be tyrants if they could. If particular attention is not paid to the ladies, we are determined to foment a rebellion, and will not hold ourselves bound by any laws in which we have no voice or representation."[2]

Alas, John Adams and the others at the constitutional convention in Philadelphia grappling with creating a new constitution paid no heed. The Constitution of the United States did not grant women the right to vote.

In 1848, at the Seneca Falls Women's Rights Convention, the most hotly debated issue was women's suffrage. Elizabeth Cady Stanton wrote in the Declaration of Sentiments that, "He [mankind] has never permitted her [womankind] to exercise her inalienable right to the elective franchise." She stated also that

---

[2] *Adams, Abigail. Letter from Abigail Adams to John Adams, 31 March - 5 April 1776. 4 pages. Original manuscript from the Adams Family Papers, Massachusetts Historical Society.*

women had long been denied access to education and the vocations. In the eyes of the law, if married, a woman was "civilly dead." "He has", Stanton wrote in the Declaration of Sentiments, "deprived her of this first right as a citizen, the elective franchise, thereby leaving her without representation in the halls of legislation; he has oppressed her on all sides." Stanton did not mince words and her anger comes through all these many years later.

New York State did act on behalf of women, passing in 1848 the Married Women's Property Act allowing married women to inherit in her own right. This law was amended in 1849. In 1860 a married woman, by law, could own any property that she had before marriage or that came to her by her own trade or labor. This law also made a married woman joint guardian of her children, with equal powers, rights and duties in regard to them. But still she had no hand in voting.

In the 1870s, women took up the pen to write essays and protested their inequality—but to no avail. In 1869, the New York Suffrage Association was formed, and in 1873, in Rochester, Susan B. Anthony voted and was then charged with violating the law. In 1878, men and women in Tompkins County submitted a petition to Albany requesting women's suffrage. That petition and many others from around the state were sent to committee but were never seen again.

In the 1890s, women of the state organized, but still there was no change. When the issue of women's suffrage was submitted to voters in 1915, it was denied. Following that defeat, and "falling forward," women began a campaign to bring the issue to the voters again. In 1917, the men of New York approved the New York State Suffrage Amendment to the New York State Constitution granting women the right to vote. Ratification of the

19th Amendment to the U.S. Constitution came on August 18, 1920, the day that the thirty-sixth state voted approval.

The 19th Amendment did not, however, give women equal rights in all things. It was federal legislation in the 1960s that finally required that all citizens have the privilege and responsibility of full citizenship.

Below is the Proclamation passed by the Tompkins County Legislature on January 3, 2017 marking the centennial of women's suffrage and also acknowledging the aspirations and contributions of the county's women. Fifty-one persons appeared in the Legislative Chambers that evening to witness the presentation of the Proclamation.

PROCLAMATION

WHEREAS, 2017 is the one hundredth anniversary of the passage in New York State of the Suffrage Act, granting women in New York the right to vote in local and state elections, and

WHEREAS, New York was the first eastern State to pass women's suffrage, an act that led to the passage of the 19th Amendment to the United States Constitution recognizing the right for women to vote across the nation, and

WHEREAS, true and full citizenship for women was not accomplished merely by achieving suffrage; for example women were not permitted to serve on juries in New York State until legislation passed in 1937, and

WHEREAS, not until federal Civil Rights legislation was passed in the 1960s were the full range of citizenship rights legally mandated to include women, and people of every and any race, and of any political suasion, as a right of that citizenship, and

WHEREAS, even today, women still must struggle for full and equal participation in the labor force and in political and economic life, and

WHEREAS, women have the right to make decisions about their lives to determine their physical and psychological well-being, yet they often suffer in a climate of sexual innuendo and/or physical harm, and

WHEREAS, the contributions of women to the progress of our nation often go unacknowledged, and

WHEREAS, if we wish to protect the rights of women in our democratic society, it is important to recognize, declare, and uphold those rights, and

WHEREAS, as the dignity of all persons must be protected, women have the right to live without fear for their physical or emotional safety and the right to pursue their own dreams in a society that recognizes their value,

NOW THEREFORE, I, Michael E. Lane, Chair of the Tompkins County Legislature, do hereby proclaim 2017 THE YEAR OF THE WOMAN IN TOMPKINS COUNTY and urge our residents to recognize and celebrate the crucial role that women of all races and ethnic and political backgrounds have played in our county's history, as well as their important place throughout our County today.

IN WITNESS WHEREOF, I have hereunto set my hand and caused to be affixed the great seal of Tompkins County, State of New York, on this 3rd day of January, 2017.

Above: Copy of Tompkins County proclamation declaring 2017 the Year of the Woman. Below: On January 21, 2017, millions of people worldwide participated in the Women's Marches around the world. The New York State Police estimated 10,000 or more turned up in Ithaca, NY. Organizers got nearly 3000 signatures from demonstrators who wanted to say, "I was here. My voice matters." Their names were on display in the Tompkins County Public Library with the Tompkins County Legislature's proclamation.

Photo credit: Carol Kammen

RACHEL DICKINSON
Walking with History

On January 21, 2017, I gave up my ticket on the bus to
Washington, DC, where I'd planned to participate in the
Women's March. Not because I didn't want to go. I gave up my
seat because I knew I had to go to the sister march in Seneca
Falls, N.Y., the little village where the American women's rights
movement began. I had to march with the ghosts of the women
and men who would be viewing the day's actions with a mixture
of pride and dismay.

I was no stranger to Seneca Falls – it's only an hour's drive
from where I live in Central New York. I took my daughter there
to hear Betty Friedan speak at the Women's Rights National
Historical Park, and the event made such an impression on her
that when her English teacher in high school asked each student
for an example of a hero, she wrote Betty Friedan's name on the
board in a sea of super-heroes. I saw Hillary Rodham Clinton
speak there when she was running for the U.S. Senate. I've been
through the exhibits at the Women's Rights National Historical
Park and read through the binders of women inducted into the
National Women's Hall of Fame. I was in touch with my
historical feminist roots.

But that still didn't prepare me for the jolt of feelings as I sat
on a hillside next to the Wesleyan Chapel and listened to speakers
invoke the sacredness of this spot – this very spot! – where
women (and some men) gathered 169 years ago to ratify the
Declaration of Sentiments, a then-radical document, which dared
to suggest that all people are created equal and endowed with
certain inalienable rights. Betty Bayer, one of the march
organizers, told me, "We are here to get a sense collectively of

how much women have done over the years." A celebration, a teaching moment, and a call to action.

When I rolled into town early on Saturday morning, the streetlights on the main street had just switched off. I wandered along the empty village sidewalks searching for coffee. The day was bright and blue-skied and promised to hit 50 degrees by afternoon, which was surely a gift. I stood on the bridge and looked at the Erie Canal, which divided the village in two, and saw the huge, brick, 19th-century Knitting Mill, which had only used wool and not cotton when it was founded so it wouldn't be contributing to the institution of slavery. The backs of the main street's brick and limestone buildings were reflected in the still waters of the canal, and it was easy to believe that 150 years had fallen away. Vees of Canada geese flew in long wavery strands overhead – a lone snow goose holding last position in one of the strands.

The rallying point between the Wesleyan Chapel and the Women's Rights Park visitors' center was filling up by the time I got there with my coffee. The chapel, site of two sweltering days in 1848 when 300 people sat in the sanctuary and argued for and then signed American women's rights founding document, the Declaration of Sentiments, had survived but only just--after serving time as a roller rink and a laundromat. I stared at the crumbly pink brick exterior and thought about Elizabeth Cady Stanton and Lucretia Mott making their case before a sweating audience, which included Frederick Douglass, Amelia Bloomer, and Mary Ann M'Clintock.

This Sister March in Seneca Falls was one of hundreds held around the country in solidarity with the Women's March being held at the same time in Washington, D.C. Planned for the day after the inauguration of Donald J. Trump as President of the United States, these marches were held in response to his election.

At the time, it was presumed that the Trump administration would gut legislation and regulations that protected women's health, enact anti-immigrant legislation, and take aim at environmental protections. Trump had proven to be crude, inarticulate, and an inflammatory speaker while on the campaign trail, and many believed he would not change while in office. Trump favored the use of words like "nasty" and "sad" when using his favorite medium, Twitter, to castigate enemies. Because Trump had shown little to no regard for women as anything other than sex objects, the Washington and Sister Marches were organized as a way to show Trump that women were a force to contend with. They could organize, show up, and represent a potentially significant voting block when riled. Many of the marchers wore pink knit caps called Pussyhats, so-called because their design made it look like the hat had two cat ears. The hats were also a not-so-subtle way to reclaim the word "pussy" that Trump had been caught on tape using when describing women he wanted to have sex with.

A sea of signs bobbed up and down as the speakers called for democratic engagement – THE FUTURE IS NASTY! SAD! RESPECT MY EXISTENCE OR EXPECT MY RESISTANCE! WE'RE ALL IMMIGRANTS! AMERICA WAKES UP– WOMEN RISE UP! IT'S OUR DUTY! TODAY IS THE CALL TO ACTION! THERE CAN BE NO BYSTANDERS IN THS MOMENT IN HISTORY! WE CAN SHAPE OUR FUTURE OR IT WILL BE SHAPED FOR US!

As women crowded into the Women's Rights National History Park that sunny January morning in 2017, a slew of speakers – poets, essayists, politicians, academics and musicians – addressed the crowd that stood with signs bobbing. All exhorted us to push hard against the mean-spirited assault against women, immigrants, the disenfranchised, and the poor that was surely headed our way.

One speaker, Mary Simpson Smart, was born in Lyons, NY, in 1915. She remembers wearing a white dress and riding in the 19th Amendment Victory Parade in 1920 in her hometown when she was five years old. Ms. Smart, a tiny person with a puff of white hair, stood at the lectern and said, "I'm just here because I'm very old. Keep standing up for women's equal rights. Carry on the way you're doing because you're doing great!"

Ten thousand people marched in the streets of Seneca Falls on January 21st, 2017, which is almost twice the population of the hamlet. We were encouraged to feel the pull of history and the deep sense of place as we marched and chanted and then packed up our signs to head home. I tried to keep the power and the spirit of Elizabeth Cady Stanton's fight for women's rights in my head as I drove along Cayuga Lake, but it was hard. I had not left the march energized but rather in despair. I believe in the power of goodness. I believe in the power of numbers. But the mean-spiritedness and the complete disregard for anyone other than wealthy white men who seemed to be sweeping through the halls of power in Washington were so disconcerting. It seemed like our country was taking giant steps backwards everywhere I looked – with women's rights, access to healthcare, protection of the environment, and protections for the poor. In choosing to march in Seneca Falls, the very place where 169 years ago the official fight for women's equality began, I was hoping to feel the power of place; to feel the determination and enthusiasm and struggle of the sisters who came before me. But for me this backfired. By taking the long view, by placing something within historical context, I was left thinking, Why do we have to keep fighting the same fight over and over again? In spite of 169 years of organized political activity, why is there still a gender pay gap? Why is women's healthcare always being determined by men? Why aren't more women in Congress and boardrooms? Why are women dismissed so easily and labeled "hysterical" when they speak out or act like men? Rather than being uplifting, this march made me realize just how ahistorical Americans are. This is the flipside of our almost irrepressible optimism. Standing there in that throng of women made me want to scream, "READ YOUR HISTORY AND DO SOMETHING!" Women have been marching for over 150 years and where are we today? Certainly not viewed as equal to men.

Thinking about all of this while driving home along Cayuga Lake threw me into the pit of despair. I pulled over and sobbed out of pent-up frustration but also in response to the beauty of nature unfolding in front of me as I clearly saw it as the metaphor for the day. I watched as a raft of snow geese – thousands of birds – lifted from the lake like a white blizzard set against the darkening sky as gray clouds knit together on the horizon. Take heed, the scene indicated, for the storm clouds are coming.

Above: The Wesleyan Chapel in Seneca Falls, restored, and now part of the Women's Rights National Historic Park, with the museum next door.

Below: Call to the First Women's Rights Convention as it appeared in the Seneca County Courier, July 14, 1848.

Images on this page courtesy of the National Park Service.

Women's Rights Convention.

A Convention to discuss the social, civil and religious condition and rights of Woman, will be held in the Wesleyan Chapel, at Seneca Falls, N. Y., on Wednesday and Thursday the 19th and 20th of July current, commencing at 10 o'clock A. M.

During the first day, the meeting will be exclusively for Women, which all are earnestly invited to attend. The public generally are invited to be present on the second day, when LUCRETIA MOTT, of Philadelphia, and others both ladies and gentlemen, will address the Convention.

NANCY AVERY DAFOE
Turning to Them Again: Recognizing Ann Carrol and Libby Smith

A faceless driver lashing the horse, her carriage raced over potholes and packed dirt, a runaway slave crouched low inside Anne Carroll Fitzhugh Smith's coach. On this night, her carriage would not be stopped, the driver not questioned, the former slave not discovered, resold, and beaten or hanged, not because Fitzhugh Smith was a woman of wealth and property, a dignified lady, but because Anne Carroll well understood the critical importance of the moment and how to act.

I reimagined this midnight scene that took place time and again in upstate New York before the Civil War after reading a new book on women's suffrage. But in the vast majority of elementary and high school texts, there is no information on Anne Carroll Fitzhugh Smith's work on abolition or women's suffrage, nor is there information on many other important women in the suffrage movement. Yet, thanks to a recent study and work, *Women Will Vote: Winning Suffrage in New York State*, by Karen Pastorello and Susan Goodier[3], we now know that Anne Carroll, who was affectionately known by the name of Nancy, was an abolitionist before she became an important suffragist.

The abolitionist and suffrage movements are inextricably linked in American history, in proximity of time and by the brave individuals taking on the social and human justice causes. The former slave on the late-night transport in Nancy's coach would be assisted in finding a place to live. Nancy would give these

---

[3] *Susan Goodier and Karen Pastorello. Women Will Vote: Winning Suffrage in New York State (Ithaca: Cornell University Press, forthcoming, 2017).*

former slaves safe passage in Peterboro, New York or other locations, time and again, always with the threat of discovery looming.

Not surprisingly, in this newly tense political climate of angry white male ascension (as if there was ever a time when white men were not at the top), I do not take New York women's voting rights for granted. But like most Americans, even the diminishing numbers who read profusely, I also do not know our suffrage history well enough.

While I may be well-read and have more than a passing familiarity with the works of Bruce Catton, David Morris Potter, Edmund Morris, Jon Meacham, Avery Craven, Michael Pye, Michael Les Benedict, John Miller, Jr., the lyrical Shelby Foote, Emory Thomas, even Doris Kearns Goodwin, I don't know enough about the roles women played in our history because their part has been understated by most historians, particularly those writing in the 19th and early 20th centuries. Americans who know their history, know only the record from a specific point of view. That view has been circumscribed by Anglo men and has largely been written as a record of white male contrivance and accomplishment, gains and losses. Gradually, more women and African American contributions are coming to light through the wider lens of contemporary historians.

As a child, I recall wishing, at times, that I, too, was a man in order to one day achieve something of lasting worth because that was the history we were fed. Women sacrificed but men achieved. I woke up to myself while still a child, but a child who had by then discovered injustice in its myriad, distorted faces and confounding figures.

When considering the question, with whom in the suffrage movement I connect, my first response would be, all of the women! Each contribution, each gesture, and brave stance made by another woman—women working alone or together with sympathetic men—led to women's right to vote in New York State in 1917. However, a general statement about suffragists also dismisses the individual contribution, the singular woman holding the curtain slightly open to check for spies outside her window, to see if the meeting place was safe, if the women's voices—talking about voting rights or the abolition of slavery—could be heard. For that reason, this comment is focused on Anne Carroll Fitzhugh Smith and her daughter Elizabeth Smith Miller.

Mother and daughter Fitzhugh Smith were, paradoxically, women of their time and completely outside it. Their exploits were astonishing. Even allowing for the collective achievements that came before this mother and daughter, the Fitzhugh Smiths moved the cause of liberty and the right to vote. If we examine the historical texts carefully, however, the recognition of their accomplishments is scarce.

Their family home in Peterboro was both safe house for the Underground Railroad and meeting place for early suffragists. An elegant soirée at the Fitzhugh Smith home was a cover for heated discussions and for planning tactics of persuasion regarding equality for blacks and women. Libby Miller and her husband later founded the Geneva Political Equality Club, but those early days must have been the most difficult and fraught with peril. How dare a woman intervene in and alter the relations of men?

Fitzhugh Smith and Smith Miller were propertied ladies who could have chosen to spend all day, every year of their lives, serving tea and stitching elegant needlework in the greatest of comforts of their time. They were, instead, activists, and they took risks.

They were subversive in the way renowned writer James Baldwin stated, "To act is to be committed, and to be committed is to be in danger," a line from his letter to his nephew, "My Dungeon Shook."[4]   Baldwin, Nancy Fitzhugh Smith, and Libby Smith Miller were separated by race, gender, and historical time, but they also shared that critically important trait of uncommon bravery in the face of gross legal and moral injustice, and a desire to effect change.

Without Nancy and Libby and other abolitionists and suffragists, Baldwin might never have written *Go Tell It On the Mountain* or *Notes of a Native Son.* Abolitionists and suffragists worked together and along parallel lines for years through the barriers of racial injustice and sexism. Nancy and Libby were individuals who made a mark. However difficult, it was just the beginning. Eradicating great oppression is a slow-moving monolith.

Libby and her daughter Anne became spokespersons for suffragists at the New York State Constitutional Convention in 1894. It seems one mother instilled activism in her daughter who found a similar will to carry the torch to the next generation: Anne (Nancy) to Libby to her daughter Anne.

While we celebrate the Centennial of women's right to vote in New York State, we should be ever mindful, looking over our shoulders and through that narrow slit in the curtains at the political weather ahead. We must be vigilant and prepared. We must also be unafraid. Although separated by time and accomplishments from earlier struggles, contemporary American women face considerable hurdles. Nancy and Libby met tall, contorted shadows and endless night with clever resolve, skillful rhetoric, and compassionate hearts. I thank them and honor their significant contributions.

---

[4] *James Baldwin. "My Dungeon—Letter to my Nephew on the One Hundredth Anniversary of Emancipation." The Fire Next Time (New York City: Dial Press, 1963).*

In May 1851 Amelia Bloomer introduced Susan B. Anthony to
Elizabeth Cady Stanton as depicted in the life-sized bronze figures
sculpted by Ted Aub, "When Anthony Met Stanton". This statue
stands in Seneca Falls. Amelia Bloomer started the first
newspaper for women, *The Lily*, which began as a temperance-
focused journal. She is also credited with advocating that women
wear the outfit that came to be known as the "Bloomer costume",
a knee-length dress with pants, as she is wearing in this statue.

Photo credit: National Parks Service

LYNN OLCOTT
Ellen Jones

There is a story in the family
about my grandmother Ellen Jones
during the nineteen-twenties
standing before a mirror in her hallway
pinning her hat to her mass of black hair
straightening her shoulders
smiling at her reflection
and going out to vote.
She was born in south Wales
came here as a child
married a tall, difficult man
had four children in six years
all of whom went to college
lived through a botched hysterectomy
cooked and cleaned for a difficult man
who drank and cheated on her
who got very ill, yet
she took care of him until he died.
Then in her seventies she moved to Phoenix
drank a beer in the afternoon now and then
subscribed to a Welsh-language newspaper
and all those years she always went out to vote.

GAIA WOOLF-NIGHTINGALL
We Always Persisted

I was not born in the United States of America. I am an immigrant.

I hail from a small Northern English village which is of little consequence except that it has the dubious distinction of being a place which was deeply embedded in Great Britain's industrial revolution in the 1800s. It was once a land of cotton mills and coal mines and it is where my journey began.

I arrived in central N.Y. on the coldest night I had ever experienced. It was a snow- covered January night. My daughter was so tired and small at just seven years old that I thought her little body would shatter from the shivers that she could not control in the frigid darkness. I look back on that day often now, as the silent snow piles deep against my window, and I reflect on my female lineage, those women who walked the sacred earth before me. How the journeys and sacrifices they made won me the right and gave me the courage to choose my own destiny.

My mother once told me the story of my great grandmother who, like me, hailed from a Northern English town named Newcastle Upon Tyne. Like my home town of Adlington, Newcastle was a busy site of industries, but instead of cotton mills and coal, Newcastle had shipbuilding and steel.

Through the great march of time my great grandmother's story became like an old jigsaw puzzle which had been left in the attic for too long, and now, though many of the original pieces had been lost, the fragments that I had were precious to me.

The story told to me began when my great grandmother was already married to my great grandfather and had emigrated to Mombasa, Kenya, just before the dawning of the twentieth century. My great grandmother was white, educated and therefore a privileged woman, but this was still a time before women's suffrage. Women in my great grandmother's era for the most part could not vote or stand for elections. It is unlikely that the idea of women's suffrage had been birthed at all in my great grandmother's consciousness as she wandered the streets of Mombasa.

As was the custom then, and as it often is to this day, women were the primary caregivers for children, and my great grandmother worked hard to raise her four rambunctious offspring. Like all hard working people she wished for breaks, for vacation time, for time to simply be. My great grandfather, a man very much of his time and generation, took himself off to the bush to hunt and explore whenever the opportunity presented itself. My great grandmother grew tired of being left alone, unable to explore the far horizons of the African plains, and so she asked her husband to take her with him on his next adventure.

My great grandfather considered this, and then explained to his wife that she could not go on safari with him because she, a woman, was of a more delicate constitution than a man. For her dignity, she would need more home comforts than he would. He did not therefore believe it would be wise for his party to carry the extra burden into the plains. My great grandmother acknowledged this.

A week later my great grandmother returned to the subject of her husband's next safari, but before he could object, she presented to him the extra guides, equipment and materials that she would require, according to his judgment.

My great grandfather once more considered, and then announced to his wife that she could not go on safari because there would be no latrine in the bush and her modest sensibilities would not be able to tolerate such an inconvenience. This was again acknowledged by my great grandmother.

Once again a week passed by and my great grandmother approached her husband on the subject of the safari. Before he could object, my great grandmother presented to him a shovel, a wooden seat and a small tent; she would have no difficulty in digging a latrine and preserving her dignity in the bush.

Again my great grandfather considered her request to go on safari with him. "Ah but what if you are in need of dentistry when out on the great plains, there will be no one to call upon for aid, if you get a toothache." My great grandmother acknowledged this.

About a week or so later, she returned to her husband and before he could formulate an objection to the subject of the safari, my great grandmother gave him a beautiful wide smile. As she did so, she revealed a shining set of false teeth. She then explained that, as she no longer had any attached teeth in her head there was no fear of her getting a toothache on safari.

My great grandmother greatly enjoyed her first safari on the African plains.

As I stumbled off the bus that had brought us from JFK airport to Ithaca and first felt the stinging embrace of that bitter cold, I was thinking of my great grandmother and her legacy. I had been afforded the privilege of coming to America because of her persistence, because of her drive to succeed and make her dreams come true, even when obstacles were constantly placed before her. She, and the millions of women like her who struggled against the prejudice of their time persisted, sacrificed and creatively found their way through the maze of barriers erected before them.

My great grandmother's spirit, and the spirit of her generation of women laid the foundation for the woman's suffrage movement. When I stepped off that bus I placed my feet on a land which was to me the epitome of that spirit. I stepped off that bus and walked in the footsteps of the women of suffrage who had walked those same streets with their placards, calling for recognition, for justice and equality.

And it is this spirit that I invoke now, as I now contemplate the US election of 2016, when for the first time in American history a woman, a pioneer of her generation, stood for election as the president. It as an election that my great grandmother would never have conceived of as she stood on the African plains.

I brought my daughter to an America where one day she may vote for the people she wishes to represent her in government, or may even stand for election herself. She will,

I have no doubt, witness a woman ascend to the office of Commander in Chief one day, and she will be able to contribute to that choice in whatever way her conscience dictates, through her vote.   This is because here in New York State in the 1800's as my great grandmother lived her adventurous life in Africa, a group of women drinking tea in Waterloo, New York, decided to make a change. They wanted the inalienable right to vote, to make their own choices about who represented them in government. A movement began, one that would require persistence, sacrifice and creativity to birth a new era for women.

A movement that gave women a voice, a stake in their own country's destiny, in their own destiny. A movement that has afforded my daughter and me, and millions of women across the globe, the opportunity to take control of our own lives. I wonder what my great grandmother would have thought of it all. I like to believe that if she could, she would have been part of the suffrage movement. She was, after all, as strong, sure, and determined as the first suffragists of England were.

I was not born in the United States of America, but I am a legacy not only of my great grandmother but also of the women of New York who began a revolution, who dared to look beyond the far horizon and see a different way of being. Perhaps as they sat drinking their tea and imagining the future of womankind, they caught the faint echo of my great grandmother's voice raised in joy at the sight of a great wildebeest migration. I like to think that they did.

MARGUERITE KEARNS
The Uphill Struggle

"Were you scared, Granddaddy, you wouldn't make a good husband for Edna?"

"I had a lot to learn when I was young," he said as I sat back in my chair and sipped orange juice.

"Like what?"

"Figuring out what I believed in, my priorities, and falling in love with Edna."

Within the next few minutes I closed my eyes and remembered Wilmer's advice: "It's as important to live inside one's self as it is to live in the outside world." By this, I figured he must have meant that my feelings, dreams, and imagination were as important as my school homework, ballet lessons, and 4-H Club sewing group. This idea was the glue in filling in the spaces of my grandfather's storytelling about being a young man working in New York City at his first job in 1903.

I wasn't there. I hadn't been born, even though storytelling doesn't distinguish between time or space or location. Storyteller and listener joined hands on a Sunday afternoon stroll when I, at age ten, accompanied my grandfather when visiting the past. The two of us headed toward Battery Park in lower Manhattan. Hikers enjoying the harbor on weekends included families, courting couples, tourists, and immigrants recently arrived through Ellis Island.

On this particular day, a young woman solicited signatures for a petition in support of votes for women. She carried suffrage literature, as well as souvenirs for sale to benefit the National American Woman Suffrage Association. When she stood on a bench to deliver a fiery speech on equality and voting rights, the message was directed to Wilmer, me, a matron and her two grandchildren. Several male passers-by shouted in the speaker's direction: "No wonder you're not married."

Public speaking about women's rights at the turn of the 20th century was risky. Those expressing public support could be splashed with buckets of water, pelted with rotten eggs, assaulted with tobacco plugs, and given derogatory names including "crowing hen," "shrieking sister" and worse. Staying out of the limelight had been part of a long-standing tradition for American women who accepted the requirements of being confined at home while men dominated the public arena. This activist had moved boldly into Battery Park to deliver her message to larger numbers of people, even if it involved facing resistance.

"Aren't you afraid for your safety?" one man called out as he passed by.

"I have every intention of acting like a modern woman even if some people still prefer the Middle Ages," she responded.

Conventional women with their hands pressed firmly around their husbands' elbows avoided walking too close to the activist. Because of her appearance, most pedestrians seemed to consider her brazen, undignified, and confrontational, unworthy of even a glance in her direction. Wilmer told me the young woman was most likely the type to bicycle through Central Park wearing a shirtwaist frock to be admired by onlookers as tall, thin, nicely proportioned with a small waist and a tumbling waterfall of brown curls down her back—elegant and eligible until she started lecturing about women's suffrage.

At the conclusion of her remarks, the young activist stepped down from the bench and headed toward Wilmer to ask him to sign a petition. He agreed, even though he claimed to know little about the movement. News of Elizabeth Cady Stanton's death two years before and the imminent retirement of her working partner

Susan B. Anthony, however, had reached Wilmer. His sweetheart Edna, my grandmother, told him the movement's success required a symbolic torch of freedom to be passed to the next generation.

The suffrage campaigner, who revealed her name as Vida, invited Wilmer to accompany her on a walk through Battery Park while she spoke about Carrie Chapman Catt and Anna Howard Shaw's movement leadership.

"I'm not familiar with Shaw and Catt," Wilmer remarked.

"They're advancing the work of Susan B. Anthony," Vida informed him.

Wilmer told me later he planned to write to Edna and tell her about the suffrage volunteer who spoke freely about how American women had made gains in terms of reforming or abolishing some of the most restrictive social legislation impacting women.

"Unfortunately the opening of some doors to women hasn't evolved to include access to the halls of power," Vida added. "Rights granted by all-male legislatures can always be taken away. Are you from around here?" she asked Wilmer.

"Beavertown. About fifteen miles from Harrisburg, the Pennsylvania state Capitol—well off the beaten track," he replied. "And you?"

"Born and raised in Brooklyn."

"Been supporting votes for women long?"

"Learned organizing from my parents who are magnets to causes. Votes for women. Prison reform. Unions. An end to poverty and war. My mother says I shouldn't be so patient with the suffrage old guard who have painted themselves into a corner by courting the Southern belles."

"What will make a difference?"

"Younger and different kinds of women joining us. We need allies of 'New Men' like you, those who won't retreat if they're called sissy or dishrag. If we have to, we'll push all the way to an amendment to the U.S. Constitution guaranteeing American women's right to vote."

"Politics can be a dirty business. What makes you so sure women voting will turn the tide?"

"We wash dirty diapers at home. We also do it in the larger household of society. We'll speak on street corners, pass out literature, meet in halls and teahouses, and continue to stand up and do whatever it takes until freedom, justice, and equality are won!"

Vida would be called a "New Woman," the type interested in more than voting rights. Many in the movement claimed voting would be the most direct route to the reforms and the power sharing they supported. Other goals included dignity, meaning, and self-respect. Wilmer's coworkers at his accounting office would refer to these women as "unsexed," those they claimed couldn't attract a man to propose marriage.

"'Women are irrational and inferior,'" Wilmer told me his colleagues remarked over a puff on a cigar and shot of whiskey when meeting in a café or saloon after work. "'It has always been this way, and it will never change because women operate with half a deck—poor things—bleeding and then carrying babies in their bellies,' men say."

Tirades like this inspired other remarks such as: "Girls are asking for trouble, dressing like they do with their chests flashing and then putting pressure on men to walk them down the aisle and take care of them. Life is hard enough for us men ruling the roost and bringing home the bacon while holding off advances from bargain-basement types.

"We civilized men better stick together, protect our families, and stay on top. We're on call constantly to perform, be in charge and fight wars so the planet doesn't spin out of control. This will happen as soon as women vote. Better keep the sexes separate—a reasonable plan humans have successfully followed for centuries. Woe to anyone who disturbs the most perfect social system ever invented."

Wilmer's work colleagues spoke about women, including their own wives, in terms of their body characteristics. They could be counted on to refer to some as "heavy set" or "curvy," note the color and style of their hair, how they dressed, and whether or not they accepted their roles of mothering, catering to men, and everything else associated with a second-class citizen role. Remarks like these were signals to young women like Edna and her friend Bess to keep a distance from the type of man who used language to devalue women.

Wilmer asked Vida's opinion as to why so many women appeared old and worn by early adulthood. "Won't voting add to women's burdens and responsibilities? And the same too if women study at universities, serve in public office, and find employment in offices and factories?" he asked.

Vida listened carefully and answered his question patiently. "Voting should be a choice. Right now, women have no choice. Some women will choose to vote. Others are what Mary Wollstonecraft called 'servile parasites,' the types who suck power from men instead of working to build power from within themselves. They're the kind to oppose women voting and anything else making females anything but barefoot and subservient."

"My friend Edna stands with you," Wilmer responded.

This story my grandfather told me barely hinted at how my grandmother Edna would develop into a firm and determined women's suffrage activist as she grew older. My mother told me on many occasions: "You can be whatever you want to be when you grow up." If my grandmother hadn't died before I was born,

I'm sure she would have shared the same message with me. The women in her generation were at the tail end of a long struggle for civil and human rights that started in fits and spurts back in 1776 and reached a turning point at the 1848 women's convention in Seneca Falls, New York, in its first wave.

"Women voting shouldn't have taken as long as it did," Wilmer said after he finished telling me the story about Battery Park in 1903. He told me other tales during the year of my tenth birthday about how American women finally won the right to vote. Wilmer marched in the men's' division of suffrage parades in New York City and Washington, DC. When my grandmother Edna traveled for state and national suffrage conferences, he stayed at home for childcare. He answered the phone to continue Edna's suffrage work. He understood that voting rights were a women's movement in which men were essential allies. After listening to Wilmer's stories, I realized all these years later that the activism of one hundred years ago is very much a part of who I am today.

It started with my grandfather's personal experiences, with me closing my eyes and holding his hand to become part of the story. I feel as if I really had been there—watching and listening to young women speaking on soapboxes, gathering names on petitions, holding rallies, and handing out leaflets. That's when our grandmothers, family members, and ancestors could only imagine a federal amendment to the U.S. Constitution. Such mighty dreams and visions they had. We have them in our DNA.

Wilmer Kearns (1881-1972) and Edna Buckman (1882-1934) on their wedding day in June 1904. After they moved to Manhattan, Edna Buckman Kearns became a suffrage activist and columnist for New York City and Long Island newspapers in the years after the birth of her first child Serena in 1905.

Photo credits: Marguerite Kearns

Edna and her eight-year-old daughter Serena Kearns are best known for the "Spirit of 1776" suffrage campaign wagon they used in New York City and on Long Island for organizing, speeches, parades and pageants prior to the 1915 NYS suffrage referendum. The "Spirit of 1776" wagon is in the collection of the New York State Museum in Albany and it is exhibited along with other suffrage movement artifacts from the period.

JUDITH SWANN
Talking Elizabeth Cady Stanton

In any discussion of white supremacy
consider what belongs to the wreck of our own
from Robinson Crusoe's ivory staff
to Stanton's love for Roxana and Moll

Even estranged from its elected leaders
white supremacy endows white women
on a class basis

and it doesn't make sense

but it explains
why she had no experience of solitary confinement
why her experience was
of being young and friendless
vis-à-vis her husband
she would not have freed my man Friday

Yet she chose to speak of solitude
having founded a movement,

a vehicle really –
not just good boots and a rain poncho –
for white women's votes

YVONNE FISHER
Election

Foremothers

Our foremothers taught us what to do. Elizabeth Cady
Stanton taught us well. She and her sisters fought for us in New
York State in the 19th century. They taught us that even when all
the forces of power are against us and we get beaten down, we
still get up and keep moving. They taught us to congregate, to
make plans and strategize. They taught us to march through the
streets, even in the rain, pelted with stones, taunted and jeered.
They taught us to keep going. They persisted. Even when kicked
and punched, arrested and imprisoned and force-fed, they kept on.
For years they rose up so that women could finally vote. They
taught us well.

Presidential Election 2016

We were all so excited and hopeful. More than hopeful,
expectant – a whole new world about to begin – the year of
women in America rising to the top, being seen and recognized,
finally having power. All the polls predicted Hillary Clinton's
win. I was nervous, of course.

But on that day I allowed myself to feel thrilled. It was a
beautiful, sunny day. Everyone was happy. Everyone wore
pantsuits. At the polls I saw good friends and they took a photo
of me at this historic moment, voting for the first woman
president. Moosewood Restaurant had a special lunch of delicious
soups for everyone to eat after voting. Everyone working there
was dressed like Hillary.

I had a celebratory lunch at Moosewood with my Italian
friends who were visiting: Luna, Titta, and Mama Lina. We ate

sweet potato soup, creamed spinach soup, white bean soup.
Everything was delicious. It felt like the beginning of a whole
new life.

Consciousness Raising

I remember learning in my early 20s that women were
oppressed. As I grew up in the 50s in a housing project in Queens,
New York, no one ever taught me that--not in school, not in the
home, not in the streets. It was just the way it was.

I was taught to be subservient, to defer to men. I learned
that when I grew older I could be a secretary or a teacher or a
nurse or a mother and wife. And that was it. We couldn't even
wear pants to school. Men had power and women had none and
that was the way life was supposed to be. Inequality was nuanced
and pervasive.

Our wave of feminism in the early '70s changed everything
for me. It all exploded and then fell into place. We started with
consciousness-raising groups – small groups of women talking
from the heart about our lives, our pain and strength, abuse and
secrets, hopes and challenges. We revealed ourselves to each
other and I had never experienced that. It was a transformative
moment of my life. We all suddenly and unconditionally began to
know each other, become allies, recognize our power, both inside
ourselves and outside, in connection to each other as we all came
together. And we began to love each other to the core. Nothing
was the same after that.

Seneca Falls Army Depot

In 1982, when I was 35 years old, I joined the Women's
Encampment in Romulus, New York, at the Seneca Falls Army
Depot–women demonstrating against nuclear arms, peacefully
and fiercely resisting the nuclear storage facility. We saw Grace

Paley, the 60-year-old feminist writer, along with so many other women, climb over the fence in peaceful civil disobedience and get arrested as we all shouted to the police: "Be gentle, don't hurt her!" She waved to us before being handcuffed.

Resistance

And now, this night, November 8, 2016, the election was going badly. It was unimaginable. We didn't yet know for sure about Russia's tampering but we knew about FBI Director Comey's interference. We knew about gerrymandering, we knew about voter suppression, and we knew that South Dakota's vote counted more than my New York State vote because of the Electoral College. We watched in disbelief as the election was being stolen. And still we hoped.

As I was watching the results come, despair set in. At one point, my Italian friends who were in the other room doing other things came into the living room and sat down on either side of me. I looked at them and they said, "We're here to support you." That's when I realized how bad it was. And, at the same time, I felt flooded with that same feeling of love and connection that I had felt all those years before. This was yet another beginning of a movement. Along with millions of others, across the nation and throughout the world, we woke up. We could not stand by and allow this to happen. We had to say No to bigotry, racism, sexism, xenophobia, autocracy, stupidity, abuse, tyranny, white supremacy and all that could come to our fragile democracy. And we were saying Yes to standing up for justice, to peacefully fighting for what's fair and right, for solidarity and for strength in our numbers.

And right then the plan began. The day after the Inauguration, millions of us would all gather together in Washington, DC, in New York City, in Ithaca, NY, and all over the country and throughout the world to demonstrate peacefully and fiercely for justice and to resist authoritarianism and oppression. It was yet another beginning. It was a continuation of all that went before. Our foremothers taught us what to do. We would persist.

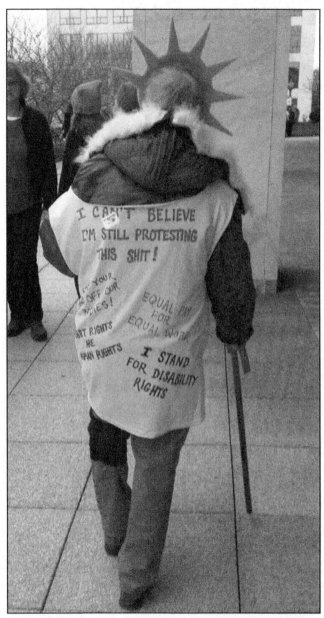

Sentiments like this were common at the Women's Marches around New York, the country and the world on January 21, 2017.

Photo credit: Alison Fromme, Ithaca NY

JENNIFER CREMERIUS
Heirloom

History tells a story—
The sepia photos and serif fonts
The marches in the streets, the word "woman"
Becoming something fearful and strong.
The resistance
Emerging quietly, like a violet in spring, shy and unsure
The persistence
Crouching in the darkness of the wood, warm and bristling.

This is my story
This is your story, child,
Its ending is unwritten.

The oak trees still stand in Seneca Falls,
The canal reflects and collects one hundred years
Of moonlight, ripples of memories inky-black and shimmering.
The roads, repaved, remember my steps.

The history of my time fills pages, edges frayed,
Scripts and scrawls clutched and damp in dainty fists.
The voices sometimes crack, the statues sometimes crack—
Our burden is our strength.

Remember me, dear child, as you face the trials of womanhood.
There is a depth behind the grainy photos,
An ending unwritten.

Part of *The First Wave* sculpture exhibit on display in the Visitor's
Center at the Women's Rights National Historical Park in Seneca
Falls, NY.

Photo credit: National Park Service

DEBORAH JONES
Women's Libber

Mother was a "women's libber" and I am, too.

Dad applied the label to my mother in the mid-1950s, before the appearance of Germaine Greer, Gloria Steinem, or Betty Friedan. Although these women took on the role of representing the women's movement in the 1960s, I feel women's liberation began more as a grass roots movement with women like my mom who were self-determining in all aspects of their lives.

My mother, Eunice R. Jones, was born in 1908 as women were fighting for their rights including the right to vote, which my mother always took very seriously. She put herself through nursing school, married and was pregnant with a daughter when her husband was killed in a car accident. Mom was a single working mother until she met and married my dad. Like so many women working outside the home, after a day at the office she returned home to take care of house, children and husband. In addition to cleaning, cooking, washing, gardening, and canning during the '50s , she helped her husband establish Jones' Cider Mill, converting our barn into one of the more popular cider mills in the area.

I recall dad calling mom "a women's libber" when I was a teenager. It wasn't totally clear to me why he called her that except it related to her working outside the home and earning more than he did. Most likely it also had to do with mom's strength of will which was there from the beginning. Upon marrying, she and Dad had bought a house needing many major repairs. Mother had sound, practical ideas about improvements, including raising the roof to accommodate dormered bedrooms. She and my dad worked together restoring the house, and as the family grew, more changes were made. One renovation I remember involved removing a weight-bearing wall separating the kitchen from the dining room. There were heated exchanges around the proposal since it required a major structural change. After a great deal of prodding, her remodeling design took shape and the cook was no longer isolated in the kitchen while others socialized in the dining room.

Early memories of my mother's projects stuck with me. When I was a graduate sculpture student, the idea came to me to renovate the old cider mill into a home and studio. On graduating, I shared the idea with my parents who showed incredible faith in the plan by deeding me the barn and an acre of land. Somewhat naïvely I jumped into fields I knew little about, construction and carpentry. However, I inherited my mother's indomitable will (and obstinacy) and I had only myself to prod to persevere in the project.

The renovation took place in the early '70s, a time when few women were in the building trades. I was fortunate to receive more encouragement than ridicule for undertaking the renovation. Mom supported my building efforts and ignored those sexist questions like, "Why does Debbie want to do men's work?" The initial makeover took me seven years. I've spent a good part of a lifetime, without regret, making improvements and correcting the mistakes and shortcomings of a naïve builder.

Thirty years after converting the family barn, I wrote about and illustrated my building adventure in a graphic memoir titled *The Barn Story*. The 56-page barn-shaped book is divided into two parts: the first half describes the process of converting the space; the second half documents the results. I created a quirky cartoon action figure as my surrogate to demonstrate how I accomplished the makeover. One page of the story describes how my mother for a birthday gift gave me a box of large C-clamps but with a delicate bracelet nestled inside. The gift was meant to express my various sides—the soft and delicate with the hard and tough!

I owe a lot to my mother; she was my champion and role model. The same goes for the many women who have inspired me by defying custom and breaking with gender restrictions to do what they felt they needed to do. This "women's libber" wrote *The Barn Story* hoping to inspire others, particularly women, to think about what they can achieve, given vision and determination.

The Age Of Iron. Man as he expects to be, by Currier and Ives, c1869, illustrating fears of the time over giving women the right to vote.

Courtesy of the Library of Congress, LC-DIG-pga-05763

"Suffrage Kewpies", a political drawing by Rose Cecil O'Neill, from 1915. *Courtesy of the Library of Congress, LC-DIG-ppmsca-40504*

Caption under pictures:
"our food, our health, our home, our schools,
Our play are all regulated by men's vote--
Isn't it a funny thing
When father cannot see
Why mother ought to have a vote
On how these things should be?"

BARBARA MINK
On Stage for Suffrage

I once spoke on the same stage as Hillary Clinton. It was at the 150th anniversary celebration of the original Women's Rights Convention in Seneca Falls on July 16, 1998. Well, I didn't really share a stage with her, more like a big tent. She spoke from the main stage as the keynoter, and I spoke in a tent devoted to women in government and journalism. As a former journalist and then-current Chair of the Tompkins County Legislature, it was a good fit. Other speakers in my area were Lynn Sherr of ABC's 20/20 and state legislators. Judy Collins sang.

Most meaningful to me was that my mother drove in from Buffalo with a favorite aunt and a few friends; she was happy to be in the presence of the First Lady, but she was mostly there for ME, as she and my father had been from the days of school plays onwards. That kind of parental support is such a luxury, one that I always took for granted, and certainly don't anymore, now that they're both gone. It's what my husband and I tried to provide for our children: showing up, as Woody Allen says, is 80% of life.

I can't find a copy of the speech I gave, but there was a paragraph in the newspaper coverage at the time: "I am a product of the second wave of the feminist revolution, born in the acquiescent '50s and growing up in the '60s. We straddled two eras and will never be free of the conflict between the messages of our childhood and the conscious choices of our adulthood." Included was more aspirational rhetoric grounded in realism, which is the way I've always worked; a pragmatism I think Hillary Clinton shares.

We had a few minutes together after the speeches, when Clinton spoke with participants and had pictures taken on the rope line. She's a few inches shorter than I am and a few years older. We talked about the challenge of raising daughters. She looks right at whoever she is talking to, none of this scanning-the-room nonsense. I was thrilled.

I admired Clinton tremendously back then, mainly for her strength in dealing with her husband's consistent bad behavior and the truly crazy hate campaigns waged against her since the beginning of her life in public. Whenever things were tough for me during my twelve years on the County Board, I would actually think, "What would Hillary do?", and it helped.

In 2008 I moved from supporting her in the presidential race to supporting Obama, a very difficult decision, but, I thought, an important one. I had never supported a woman for office just because of gender; there are too many examples of how that is no indication of progressive beliefs or ability to enact policies to effect change. In this last shocking election of 2016 I didn't have much trouble supporting Bernie Sanders in the primary, with the hope of getting Clinton and the Democratic establishment to acknowledge and deal with the economic and societal inequalities that are dividing this country more than political affiliation.

I knew, of course, that I would vote for Clinton and, when she won, the battle would continue in the way it always had, moving incrementally forward.

The reality we face now is almost impossible to understand, since there is no historical precedent in my lifetime that can serve as a guide. But I come back to the conclusion of Clinton's speech almost twenty years ago, which I find more resonant than ever:

"The future, like the past and the present, will not and cannot be perfect. Our daughters and granddaughters will face new challenges which we today cannot even imagine. But each of us can help prepare for that future by doing what we can to speak out for justice and equality for women's rights and human rights, to be on the right side of history, no matter the risk or cost, knowing that eventually the sentiments we express and the causes we advocate will succeed because they are rooted in the conviction that all people are entitled by their creator and by the promise of America to the freedom, rights, responsibilities, and opportunity of full citizenship."

No matter how our opinions or approaches might differ on some issues, I will always be grateful to her for being a strong, resolute, and focused role model for women everywhere.

Barbara Mink and Hillary Rodham Clinton, July 5, 1998, Seneca Falls NY.

Photo courtesy of Barbara Mink

SARAH JEFFERIS
Calling for Ancestors

To welcome all the selves,
to welcome Winstensteins who changed to Winston
at Ellis Island.
To welcome menorahs on pianos, china platters wall hung.
To welcome the food scientist, the interior decorator,
the Canadian professor who will not call me niece;
to welcome a synonym of a father, a musician who left on the
count of three—
To welcome the other tree,
to welcome the family farm in Shippensburg
to welcome quilters who hung the right patterns on railings
to welcome the underground railroad
to welcome a worn path between spring house and barn,
to welcome daughters of a pastor who fought to vote,
whose cheek bones reappear on my own daughters,
to welcome a pants-wearing, bourbon-drinking grandmother
who loved women and sometimes men,
who as a pregnant unmarried champion swimmer
dropped my mama in a basket on cathedral steps
for the nuns in Philly.
To welcome the scrapple-making great aunties
who were too late for the basket baby
but instead arrived for the nine-year-old girl:
my mama fluent then in Latin and French
though never once stepped in a school.
To say I am from you and you and you
I will not turn my face to the wall
will not cross myself

will have the lesson of hiding
will memorize the script of leaving
of night-running in the blood.

Suffragists posting bills to get out the right to vote, 1912.
Photo courtesy of the Library of Congress, LC-USZ62-22260

ERICA S. BRATH
Pain, Perseverance, and Intersectionality

War is not healthy for children and other living things is embroidered
on the jeans I wore as a toddler. I imagine my mother sewing
them for me, a Kent golden light burning in a nearby ashtray. She
drove a Camaro to and from shifts as a nurse; under the kitchen
sink there was always a bottle of stark white shoe polish, which
she'd use on her wedge-heeled shoes with the blue heart on the
heel. Her starched white nurse's hat was in a box in the upstairs
closet.

My grandmother, her mother, was also a product of her time,
spending her life as a homemaker—cooking, baking, cleaning,
raising kids—while my grandfather worked, first in the coal
mines of western Pennsylvania, and then running the rock
crusher at a concrete plant. My grandmother didn't smoke, didn't
drink, was staunchly Catholic; the ubiquitous framed Jesus
painting with eyes that followed my every move hung in the
stairway. She didn't even drive; she'd given that up at some point
before my time. She married into a big Polish family, and made
everything from scratch, including the traditional Christmas Eve
dinner, when every member of the family packed into my
grandparents' tiny two-story house in a suburban New Jersey
neighborhood that used to be a chicken farm.

An assortment of family photos adorned the walls, including
a large, oval-framed photo of my maternal great-grandparents'
wedding in May, 1924: him in a dark suit with a white flower in
his lapel, her with short, bobbed hair, her dress falling mid-calf.
Her wedding attendants are dressed in the same style, with
headbands with large flowerlike poufs off to one side. They are all
flappers.

My great-grandmother's parents came from Hungary, and according to my grandmother, were Romani, or Gypsies. I'm not entirely sure that's true, but it certainly adds a romantic notion to what was, in reality, an extremely difficult life.

My great-grandmother was widowed at 46 and never remarried, living life on her own terms for the next three decades—or as close to her own terms as a middle-aged widow of a coal miner was allowed. She made quilts of varying patterns, depending on how deep into her evening libations she was; she raised backyard chickens, one of which might find itself killed, plucked and in a pot by the end of the day.

In my memory, my great-grandmother is a large woman with a tight, steel-grey bun perched high atop her head, small wire glasses, and what in those days was called a house dress. We'd visit her occasionally outside Hazleton, Pennsylvania. I remember very little of her home, and even less of her previous one, which had an outhouse and wood-fired oven. But she always seemed happy, kind, and opinionated. The one visit I remember clearly involved an argument between her and my mother about getting my ears pierced, which she defended and my mother staunchly prohibited. I was in middle school and wanted to be like my friends. She was my hero that day.

Growing up, I was well aware of the women who came directly before me, and the roles they played. They were mothers, homemakers, job holders, hard workers, each playing out a life society deemed acceptable for them as they did their damnedest to hold their families together, raise kids, and have joy for themselves at the end of the day.

And thanks to them and other strong women before me, I am free to be nothing like them.

I cast my first presidential vote in 1992 for Bill Clinton, when he was running against the old money George H.W. Bush, who liked to summer in New England and who famously couldn't figure out how to purchase a pair of socks.

I'd just entered art school near the dead center of New York State, a post-industrial town that boasted a brewery and little else. I was 21, and had just restarted my college career, having completed a year at two separate state universities—one in Massachusetts and one in North Carolina, along with a failed third semester where teenage me decided working part-time at a hardware store, deejaying at the local college radio station, and going to see bands play was preferable to the rigors of academia. I'd finally decided school was the answer after my fourth year of working for $3 to $4 an hour at a series of spirit-crushing part-time jobs, doubling-up just to pay the rent. I'd spent the summer as a temp at the local town office, where I was treated with a combination of amusement and innuendo by those coming in and out, mostly road crews and maintenance men. They thought I was cute, entertaining, but the only respect I earned was from the women I worked with, although they did warn me that my voice was "too sexy" when I answered the phone.

It was the first presidential election I was old enough to participate in and, like so many people my age, I thought it was important. I'd seen my future under the Republicans—I'd spend my entire life in struggle under the governance of those totally out of touch with the working class. I'd also watched Congress, led by Senator Jesse Helms, try to gut the National Endowment for the Arts over Robert Mapplethorpe's homoerotic nudes, and the thought of such right wing conservative overreach into something as sacred as freedom of expression, something I'd chosen to dedicate my life to, seemed like the end of the world.

Ironically, I don't actually remember casting a vote, but I do remember the journey my roommate and I took on a pitch black night driving winding roads in far upstate New York to get her to the polls on time. She was from Plattsburgh, near the Canadian border, and if absentee ballots were an option it was lost on us. Our days were spent memorizing names and dates of art and artists in between part-time jobs to pay the rent.

So we hopped in her brown 1980s sedan and headed north just as the sun was setting. Pre-internet, we relied on her memory to navigate the horror-story-worthy roads that ran through the Adirondacks, backtracking more than once. Pulling up to her polling place a few moments before it closed, we felt as if we'd run a marathon. Our duties as citizens fulfilled, we stopped at her parents' house to raid the fridge before heading back to our apartment and daily lives. We were elated the next day to learn our candidate had won. We didn't realize then that hitting the booth every four years wasn't enough.

I have fleeting memories of voting in presidential elections since—in an auditorium in San Francisco's Chinatown, someone's living room in West Philadelphia town buildings, fire halls, fire stations, and community rooms. And while the results have not always gone the way I've wanted, only Bush v. Gore ignited anything resembling the apocalyptic nuclear reaction I've experienced since the November 2016 election.

This was more than just an election to me. It felt like a referendum on the very act of being female.

The suffragists held the first Women's Rights Convention in 1848 to protest their legal status as second-class citizens. Their ineligibility to vote, own property, or determine the paths of their lives was as enshrined as their role as members of subservient of society. They were up against a solid legal roadblock and their goal was simple: to dismantle it, forcing the constitution to endow them with the same rights as men.

While my roommate and I navigated those dark roads all those years ago, we had little idea what the women before us, who gave us the right to vote, and even to own and drive our own cars, endured securing those rights. We were attending school 96 miles from Seneca Falls, New York, engaged in learning, literally, about the art that reflected and sometimes shaped society in the past and present. But the history we'd been taught regarding the Women's Rights Movement was watered down, sliced and diced and pared to fit into a narrative drained of both substance and scale, when in reality it encompassed both. We were fed a story of a sign-toting Mona Lisa. The reality was closer to Gentilieschi's Judith.

George Orwell wrote, "The most effective way to destroy people is to deny and obliterate their own understanding of their history."

British suffragettes blew up buildings, attacked politicians, even set an entire train aflame, leaving suffragist literature behind in the still-smoldering ashes. But the violence wasn't one-sided: countless women were jailed for their guerrilla activities, thrown in solitary confinement, and force-fed.

Here in the U.S., suffragists' determination was no less intense. Alice Paul spent time in prison in England for her suffragist activities before using some of the same tactics in the U.S., although outright violence was frowned upon by many of the American suffragists themselves. They preferred pageantry, persistence, and making themselves a constant presence in the eyes of their fellow citizens. And they paid for their audacity to demand equal status.

The first Women's March took place in 1913 on the eve of Woodrow Wilson's inauguration, led by Inez Milholland Boissevain astride a white steed, clad in white robes. Eight thousand women marched, with angry mobs attacking them throughout the route.

Suffragists picketed outside the gates of the White House starting in January, 1917, despite continued physical attacks at the hands of other Americans and the police. World War I was underway and protesting was seen as un-American. In total, 168 women were arrested and sent to Occoquan Workhouse, subjected to beatings and force feedings three times a day. Lucy Burns' hands were handcuffed to her cell above her head all night on November 15. Unable to pry her mouth open, guards shoved a glass feeding tube up her nose.

Alice Paul and Rose Winslow began a hunger strike on November 5, 1917, to protest this brutality. New York gave women the vote the next day, the first eastern state to do so.

Women were imprisoned, beaten and abused just for demanding equal rights. Yet the history of the women's movement I was taught while growing up was little more than a passing mention, despite the fact that I was surrounded by it: my parents built a home seven miles from Peterboro, New York, where the Underground Railroad, antislavery, suffrage and reform activities of Gerrit Smith, a noted abolitionist, politician and philanthropist, took place. Smith's cousin, Elizabeth Cady, met her husband, Henry Stanton, in Peterboro.

And until this year's Women's March, the issue of race and the suffrage movement's largely racist past wasn't even touched upon in any real way in the history I was taught. No mention was made in my high school history classes of the fact that Frederick Douglass was a staunch believer in the movement, supporting Elizabeth Cady Stanton and participating in the first Women's Rights Convention in Seneca Falls. And yet, Stanton's abhorrent prejudice is clear. In regard to giving male slaves the vote, Stanton wrote, "I would not trust him with all my rights; degraded, oppressed himself, he would be more despotic with the governing power than even our Saxon rulers are."

Many of the Suffragists who spent so much time and energy fighting for female equality deemed African Americans second-class to even their own discriminated-against class. Their version of inclusion was upper crust and white.

In fact, the issue divided the suffragist movement. In 1869, the American Women Suffrage Association (AWSA), founded by activist Lucy Stone, split from the National Women Suffrage Association (NWSA), founded by Susan B. Anthony and Elizabeth Cady Stanton, due to the latter's belief that abolition of slavery via the ratification of the 15th Amendment should not come before giving women the right to vote. Even the first Women's March in 1913 was a segregated event, with women of color at the back of the procession. Despite their gains, suffragists failed their gender, their allies, and society at large in this crucial respect.

The road to the women's vote was an ugly, blood soaked, blister-inducing, discriminatory slog that took years. It was at turns boring, abhorrent, time-intensive and awe-inducing. It was not, however, the white-clad bonneted pinkie-raised tea and petits fours party we'd been led to believe. Had we been told the truth, we might have understood the hard work still ahead of us in order to see the first woman vie for the Oval Office a century after women across the U.S. forced our government—using every tool and ounce of determination they could muster—to allow us to vote nationwide.

The suffragists were starkly human, deeply flawed human beings who stood firm in their beliefs, even when those beliefs were reprehensible. They continued despite being pushed back and brutalized, eventually securing their ultimate goal. They built the foundation we stand upon and learn from. And yes, parts of it we must reject if we are to move forward.

But it is the foundation we build from—and work to improve, together—today.

Above: Wedding Photo of Mary Schauer and John Wisda, 1924.

Left: Three generations of strong women: the writer's mother, Mary (Winchock) Brath (held), grandmother Eleanor (Wisda) Winchock (holding baby) and great great grandmother, Maria (Simshick) Schauer, circa 1947.

YAEL SAAR
Alternative Facts Universe

The Foundry of the Alternative Universe Foundation was quiet
and cool. All forging and casting equipment had been removed
long ago; their holographic imprints decorated the south walls
along with descriptions of the abandoned arts of metal casting
and welding. The only sparks here were mental, the only thing
being cast were spells. The Smiths who ran it were overseers, not
makers, charged with observing and monitoring the unfolding of
countless experiments in free will, life force, greed, and love.

A Smith noticed an aberration: the pain scale for Alternative
Universe (AU)104.04XT1125.0820 was at "smoldering" levels.
This meant that their Scriptors, a trio of young men in the
second-to-lowest circuit, had gotten themselves into the hot
water of an ethics audit.

The world under examination was a standard carbon-based
third rock, one dominant species: oxygen-dependent humanoids,
only two widely recognized genders. It was still in the early
social stages, as could be deduced from the presence of separate
"nations". It wasn't clear if this world could reach the next stage,
as it was climbing towards its boiling point faster than it was
evolving.

In this AU (Alternative Universe), the Scriptor team was
given several exemptions from Standard Foundry Protocols. The
laws of abundance were scaled back two notches; the vectors of
greed and fear were amplified one notch each. The Scriptors were
afforded congruence exemptions, including the requisite
heightened levels of suspension of disbelief. The project's special
effects budget was laughably small, mainly because it was a well-
known phenomenon that in constellations where greed was

allowed to have the upper hand, nature invariably retaliated spectacularly.

"You couldn't make this shit up!" said the youngest Scriptor, slapping his knee.

"Well, you could, but then nobody one would fund your plotline," another one sneered, "and yet, here we are."

The Smith knew the banter was not meant for her ears but that didn't make it excusable any more than "locker room talk." She wondered, What are Scriptors being taught at the academy these days? And how are they being screened? She blinked twice to form a mental note to look into the admissions protocols.

They didn't notice her until she was right there, clearing her throat. They looked up at her, startled.

"Young men, the suffering signal from the world in your care activated the Smith Ethics Mandatory Review process. We have concerns about your choices, their effects on your worldlings, and last but not least, on the quality of your plot and narrative. So I'll start with that: take for example the brouhaha at the largest democracy in your test planet's Western Hemisphere. The trick about the Electoral College versus the popular vote was intriguing the first time, but using it again in favor of the same political party just seems lazy. Can't you think of any other plot devices for mayhem?"

"We are perfectly within rules. Nothing says we can't resort to any tool as many times as we like," insisted the head of the team.

The youngest one, emboldened by the team leader's response, couldn't resist a pun. "I think we should 'resort' more often. Maybe R&R at some fancy hotel on a tropical beach would cause a surge of originality." His laughter was cut short by her raised eyebrow. He blushed brightly, looked down, fidgeted with the comlink tattoos on his wrist.

"Being within guidelines is not necessarily the same as making good or ethical use of them. What would it take to get a surge of real creativity from your team?" She rested her gaze briefly on each one of them, then fixed it on the team leader. "Look, you've been horribly creative in the way you've experimented with war design, and your environmental collapse trajectories are yielding some interesting measurements that corroborate existing theories, but the high degrees of sexism and racism you are employing is veering off the deep end. A lack of subtlety is common with young single-gender Scriptor teams, but it doesn't have to be. Don't let it compromise your work."

She paused to let her words sink in. "You are taking your exemptions too far. You were allowed to experiment with colonialism, capitalism, racism, and other "isms", so the resulting wars, terrorism, disease, rising toxicity and food shortages are not surprising. But female genital mutilation? Seriously? This is the only Alternative Universe in all of TimeSpace where this monstrosity exists. Which one of you came up with that one?"

They all looked at their shoes, but she could tell. She always could.

"A sexual predator defeating the first female presidential candidate in the largest democracy in your care is not irony, it's bathroom humor. Why of course, seeing that the ridiculous figure of speech 'locker room talk' will have come from your creation just strengthens my point. This is not nearly as amusing as you think. Don't let the plotline exemptions you've been afforded erase your ethical or aesthetic standards. The suffering experienced by sentient beings in your care should only be in the service of scientific observations and the greater GOOD! Every choice you make has far-reaching butterfly effects, most of which you are not advanced enough in your education to fully comprehend or measure accurately. There is always room for humor in scripting, but frankly, having 'Alternative Facts' be a trend in an Alternative Universe, and making 'suffragists' suffer, are bad puns, not comic relief."

The Smith could not deny that what was often called God had a peculiar sense of humor, but she had lost her tolerance for juvenile Scriptors jokes.

She turned to face the table and her attention activated the holographic viewer: time coordinates: 1917; space coordinates: Seneca Falls, N.Y., USA. The boys blinked and swallowed, practically in unison. How did she know to go directly to this point in TimeSpace that they couldn't explain or suppress?

She zoomed in on white women dressed in black, walking single file holding signs. They almost appeared to be in uniform; they obviously belonged to the same socioeconomic group-- which in her long experience was an indicator of futility. Revolutions didn't become evolutions without intersectional collaborations. She sighed. No wonder it took a whole century to get a female to the top of their presidential ticket.

She looked up and down the timelines, then sideways across geographic locations. Apparently the state of New York matched the audit algorithm for a representative sample for her observations. The main port of entry to the largest immigrant nation on the planet was decorated by a huge yet pleasing statue they called "Lady Liberty." Interesting skyscrapers; she was familiar with the "Chrysler Building," universally famous as a rare example of tasteful phallic architecture. The Twin Towers and their aftermath elicited the familiar shoulder tension in reaction to senseless violence. Smiths who stopped experiencing this psychophysical reaction were supposed to report its absence as a sign of burnout.

The Smith spent another minute randomly looking around, making a mental note to go back to look at the "Woodstock" and

"Grassroots" festivals; those looked like fun. She'd take them in with her tea later.

She was brought back to Seneca Falls a hundred years later. In 2016, a century after New York women started their protests and marches, their stomping grounds had been turned to memorials and museums. The suffragists' stories were on display, their graves were reverently marked. In the weeks before the elections women made pilgrimages to them, placing oval "I voted" stickers on their graves. The resting place of a woman named Susan B. Anthony, in Rochester, N.Y., showed up in countless "selfies" and short movies shared on the nascent global electronic networks, starting "#hashtags." Sweet, really. In other parts of the state, the country, and in the rest of the world, women held their breath in anticipation, but then had their hopes crushed.

Focusing on the weeks after the 2016 USA elections more closely, here was the Electoral College taking center stage again. An avalanche of phone calls, letters, demonstrations, and "tweets" called on that constitutional college to serve its intended purpose, but to no avail. The Scriptors didn't have to actively push the electors into choosing party over country in defiance of their constitutional mandate to protect their "United States" from autocracy and fascism. She was not surprised; greed did this to systems. This was another data point for her theory that it was no longer productive or ethical to drag universes through experiments of this line of thought. Not enough learning remained in that arena to justify the suffering. She'd have to speak up when the Universal Ethics Congress convened again. It might be wise to coordinate this with other like-minded Smiths.

She turned to watch the poorly attended 2017 presidential inauguration and the historically large Women's March the following day. This time she liked what she saw: funny pink hats atop heads and faces of all ages, all colors, all genders. Many cultures appeared on the display. Women were singing songs, holding hands, hugging, drumming. And those "selfies" again. She chuckled and scrolled sideways. Marches like this were in full swing all over that globe.

She glanced at the team members. The three young men didn't show any signs of awareness that they were just as much the subjects of this experiment as were the humans wearing "nasty women" t-shirts, the hordes making phone calls to their representatives, or the corporate executives bribing those same officials. She found this lack of awareness depressing; it was the same disappointment she felt when observing those willing to jeopardize their entire ecosystems trying to generate or hold onto power. Earthlings that had no way of knowing that there was, in fact, an endless supply of control-group planets and universes, were recklessly compromising the life support systems of the only planet their kind would ever have access to.

And here, similarly, the Scriptors were blind to the fact that their choices would determine the rest of their careers, the rest of their lives. And for what? It couldn't be just for the jokes. Something was off.

She took a deep breath, opened her mouth to speak, then said nothing. Only a few minutes of Alternate Universe Foundry time had gone by while she took in a whole century of events. She felt a tightness behind her eyes. She turned off the screen with a blink, but didn't fully terminate the mental link. She could continue to observe the unfolding of (AU)104.04XT1125.0820 anytime, anywhere. A Smith of her rank had the skill to return to the specific open mental tab with just a tiny shift of her attention. She'd have to remember to deliberately sever the connection to this experiment when the audit was complete. She made her parting words brief and bland; further input from her could taint the data needed for their performance evaluation.

Instead of walking straight back to the Smith's Bridge she took a walk through the gardens. Species of flora and fauna from all over TimeSpace were given the conditions to flourish in controlled environments. She let herself into her favorite one, found her usual bench, and removed her shoes to wiggles her toes in the warm sand, closing her eyes to feel the warmth of the setting sun.

She recalled the indignation on the faces of the three young men. These teams never liked audits. Who could blame them? She turned her attention back to the open tab in her mind, to the stage in the experiment where her own research interest lay: the turning points where the will of the scriptors lost its power.

She winced. What a mess! And yet, for every cruel executive order, for every power-grab bill passed by the House of Representatives, for all the threats to the freedom of speech, immigration, or health care, she noticed reactions that sparked her hope: people getting together in town hall meetings, listening circles, postcard parties, rallies at airports, marches, sit-ins. People nourishing each other by sharing homemade food, childcare, song and poetry, offering support and plotting ways to preserve their democracy. Even the suspension of the Law of Abundance at the hands of a single-gender Scriptor team couldn't quell that.

She smiled, set her internal meditation session to one hundred breaths. When the end-of-meditation shudder arrived, she opened her eyes and tapped quickly at her wrist to place an order.

Just a few hours later, the package arrived via WormHole Express. The contents: an original (No hologram, no ExactoReplica!) hand-knitted pink hat with the words "And Nevertheless She Persisted" embroidered in white, and a round metal button pin with the image of Lady Liberty sporting an "I voted" sticker. She palmed the relics with satisfaction. She would donate both items to the Universal Free Will Museum when the time came, but for now she enjoyed the tactile pleasure of the warmth of the hat, the coolness of the pin: the hard and soft proof that some things could never be explained or suppressed.

Above and Below: Photos from the January 21, 2017 Women's March in Ithaca, NY.

Photo credit: Lauren Loiacono.

KATHARYN HOWD MACHAN

How to Reach an Understanding of One Aspect of Feminism

Watch a woman alone in a restaurant
sitting at a small table waiting to eat.
If two men are seated near her
they will glance over, appraise, glance again
if she is young and normal and pretty.
What is a woman doing alone
young and pretty in a restaurant
when there are so many men
hungry for companionship?
Why does she sip her water calmly
gazing out the window, calmly waiting,
unflurried by their glances?
Is she sick? Is she perhaps
not normal, deficient in some important way?
The men begin to grow uneasy,
shift in their chairs, wonder if maybe
they are not quite up to snuff.
Soon she will occupy herself with eating
comfortably, and seems not to have noticed
them at all. Gall! Impertinence.
The men speak of none of this.
It all happens within moments.
The woman is fully aware
she is angering them, and understands
the men will leave the restaurant despising

her: stuck-up broad, cold bitch,
not so very pretty anyway.

She will remain, sipping coffee,
a woman who knows the proper games
and defies propriety, and refuses
to suffer over that fact anymore.

Watch her.

"Swallow Your Pride": Painting by Judith Galgoczy, Ithaca NY,
2016

SALLY ROESCH WAGNER, PhD
LET'S GET MILITANT!

Speech Delivered at New York Cultural Heritage Tourism Network, Women's Suffrage Centennial Conference, October 7, 2016

This is a time of great potential, a celebration of significance. The U. S. government was founded on a vision of rule by the people – not a monarch or a ruling elite but each person with a voice, a vote. But 144 years later, half the people still were not recognized in the constitution as having a voice.

State by state, women carved out a voice – in school, municipal, finally state government. New York in 1917. But federally women were still silenced.

The 19th Amendment was finally ratified in 1920 guaranteeing women suffrage. It has rightly been called the Second American Revolution.

There is a great potential to create a major national celebration in 2020, comparable to the blockbuster 1976 Bicentennial, when the nation focused a year celebrating the first American Revolution. This one could be as big.

But the greatest likelihood from all the signs, is that it will be a huge ho-hum; a lost opportunity. Why?

Part of it is the story we have to tell. The dominant narrative is this: Susan B. Anthony and Elizabeth Cady Stanton led women in asking for the vote for 72 years and were finally given it. This is the story adults know and students are still learning today. Frankly, this story stinks like old cheese. It has no guts, no passion no relevance. It's disempowering. Does a young girl see herself in it anywhere? It's yesterday's news.

Women are shamed into voting: "You have a responsibility to vote because your foremothers worked so hard for you to have this right." This is just a collective version of the old "I worked my fingers to the bone for you."

And it's not even the real story. Sit in a yearly national woman's rights convention in the 1850s and hear demands for equal pay and an end to violence against women. Attend a National Woman Suffrage Association convention in the 1870s to fight for a woman's right to control her own body and make her reproductive choices. Read Matilda Joslyn Gage's book in 1893 and learn about the sexual abuse of children by priests and the terrible problem of sex trafficking.

Watch the merger of the suffrage groups in 1890 and see this multi-issue, grass roots movement collapse into an authoritarian, single-minded focus on the vote, systematically tossing all the other issues of women's oppression aside like so much excess baggage.

In the 1850 conventions you will sit beside blacks and whites, free lovers and social conservatives, atheists and Christians. But by 1900 you may belong to a segregated state affiliate of the National American Woman Suffrage Association, making the argument to men that they should give women the vote because white women outnumber blacks and immigrants and woman suffrage is the way to maintain white, native-born supremacy. Or you may be a member of a Black Woman Suffrage Association. You may listen to your minister preach an anti-suffrage sermon citing Biblical passages proving that God decreed that women should be under the authority of men; women voting will destroy the family and ultimately Western civilization. Or you may be a Freethought member opposing woman suffrage because you fear the agenda of the largest women's organization, the Woman's Christian Temperance Union. They are working to get the vote so they can put God in the constitution and set up Jesus Christ as the head of the government–destroying the wall of separation between church and state and creating a fundamentalist religious government.

You may find your model of how women should be treated in your nearby neighbors, the Haudenosaunee, the six Native Nations where women have an equal voice in government, body right, and spiritual agency.

This story has agency, conflict, relevance, passion – it's sexy. It makes us wonder, if we didn't know this, what else don't we know? It creates a hunger for more history, more truth in history. But it's a story that probably won't be told over the next three years. Why? Because women are marginalized. In 2012 the New York State legislature budgeted $450,000 for events commemorating the War of 1812. In 2016 the New York State legislature budgeted $500,000 for events commemorating the entry of one-half the population into political life. That is the best they could come up with in their $90 billion budget. We are as important as one single men's war.

We are eternally grateful for crumbs. Despite our marginalized funding over and over we get things done. We do it if it needs to be done and we do it on a shoestring. We are the bake sale queens.

Let's reverse our thinking. Let's think big. Let's think about what we could do with $12,548,710.60 — the cost of one drone, a single MQ-9 Reaper unmanned aircraft. The Air Force ordered 10 of them. Let's tell them: Get by with nine.

What could we do with $12 and a half million dollars?

Let's start with sites: where it happened. As Sen. Betty Little said at the founding meeting of the New York State Woman Suffrage Centennial Commission, "What if we bring all these visitors to the suffrage houses and they're in a state of disrepair?" I ask further, "What if the lights aren't on?" Most of our houses and sites operate on half a shoestring. We need to begin with the physical infrastructure of our story. Make sure it's sound. Fill the sites with interactive, state of the art exhibits and innovative programs that launch dialogues about the remaining issues of women's rights.

How about New York hosting a women's rights summit, bringing together clan mothers, African-American, Latina, Asian-American, immigrant women and activists to shape the women's rights agenda for 2020 onward? Let's talk about who doesn't get to vote today and why.

Let's identify more sites: Continue Judy Wellman's identification project of all the state's women's rights sites. And Tom Flynn's identification of now 83 Freethought sites in NY, an overwhelming number of them closely associated with women's rights.

Let's fund the women's rights trail and the new Underground Railroad consortium. Let's fund Ganondagan and the Skan-Nonh Center to tell the story of how suffragists learned what it meant to be equal from Haudenosaunee women. Hire scholars to build on the new scholarship that is pulling all these elements together and blowing the old, tired story to pieces, then hire them to share their richly-textured stories and work with the sites to develop a coherent, integrated women's rights story, with a piece of it at each site. Let's link the full story of the integration of women's rights, abolition, Native American, and religious freedom in a major tourism initiative.

History lies dormant in every village, town and county, like a Pandora's box. Open that box and--watch out. Partner with teachers to work with students digging through newspapers to uncover the women's rights story in their town. Pay historical societies to mine their collections, those boxes of stuff nobody's had time to go through, and we'll uncover treasures, like the superb collection of woman suffrage posters in the Howland Stone Store Museum–and the piece of Susan B. Anthony's birthday cake they have!

Let's fund a grass roots, state-wide history project to get every community involved in discovering its stories, claim its part in this transformation of society. Let's repopulate history, bring it alive and share it.

We are the real birthplace of Democracy, on the shores of Onondaga Lake where the Five Haudenosaunee Nations before Columbus created the world's oldest continuing democracy in the world, the model for our own government.

We have the suffragists and women's rights activists–from the National Woman Suffrage Triumvirate: Anthony, Stanton and Gage–whose homes are equidistant from each other off Interstate Route 90--a magnet for tourism. We have the Civil War heroes Mary Walker and Harriet Tubman; the first ordained women ministers, Antoinette Brown Blackwell (irregularly ordained) and Olympia Brown (her ordination recognized by her denomination). We have the richest landowner in the state of New York, Gerrit Smith, who used his wealth to fund every social justice cause in upstate New York, which was the hotbed of radical reform. We have Victoria Woodhull, that communist stockbroker and Belva Lockwood, the first woman lawyer to plead a case before the Supreme Court, both of whom ran for President before women could vote.

You know what Nicholas Kristof and Sheryl WuDunn reported in *Half the Sky*? When international funding is given to men, they're inclined to spend it on hookers and booze. Give the money to women and they spend it on education, health, and building the community. Upstate needs economic development.

And the state government threw money at it. You know what we got when New York State gave money to men to develop upstate's economy? Felony charges of rigged bids, extortion and bribes. A $15 million state-of-the-art film studio that sits vacant. $90 million for a manufacturing facility whose construction may be shut down because of the corruption case. Give a fraction of that money to fund women's rights and we WILL develop upstate economically. And we won't end up in jail.

This is a moment when we can make history relevant. Women demanded "Equal Pay for Equal Work" as early as the 1850s, when women made half the wages that men made. One hundred and fifty years later and we've barely turned the corner on 75%. Are we ready to wait another 150 years for the other 25%?

Healing can take place now, as well. We can celebrate our victories and progress, but we also have an opportunity to practice Truth and Reconciliation. Strong connections existed between the anti-slavery and woman's rights movements before the Civil War. The passage of the 14th amendment, which defined citizenship as exclusively male, and the 15th amendment which gave African-American men voting rights, split the two movements. The well-documented organizational racism of the National American Woman Suffrage Association (NAWSA) after 1890 and the later Woman's Party (WP), both of which played the race card to win the right to vote, involved allowing their state organizations to segregate, making African-American women march at the end of their parades, and asking allies like Frederick Douglass not to attend conventions held in the South. Acknowledging this legacy of racism could begin healing this long-festering wound. It's time.

The movement we're commemorating was messy and it was militant. It was illegal for women to vote, and these suffragists broke the law by voting in droves. They impeached the government for its treatment of women in 1876, saying they had more cause for revolution than the founding fathers, and risked arrest when they illegally presented their Declaration of Rights of Women at the official Centennial Celebration.

They chained themselves to the White House and called out President Wilson for fighting for democracy across the ocean while denying it to women at home. We honor these women lightly by voting but we honor them deeply by picking up the issues they began, demanding full equality and self-determination in every part of our collective lives.

They worked to get constitutional protection for the vote for 72 years. We picked up their issue and have worked for equal rights to be guaranteed to women in the constitution for 93 years and we still don't have an equal rights amendment! And to add insult to injury, the U.S. is the only democracy that has not ratified CEDAW, the International Bill of Rights for Women.

Will we enter 2020 an embarrassment in the eyes of the world because the U.S. arrogantly demands human rights from other countries while refusing to recognize equal rights for women in our own country?

When New York suffragists demanded and won the right to vote in school elections in 1880, Governor Lucius Robinson vetoed the bill, declaring that the God of Nature did not intend women for public life. When he ran again for governor, the women resolved that the same power should retire Mr. Robinson from public life. They defeated him and the next governor promptly signed the bill. Matilda Joslyn Gage, who led the fight, left us this message in 1880: "When men begin to fear the power of women, their voice and their influence, then we shall secure justice, but not before. When we demonstrate our ability to kill off, or seriously injure a candidate, or hurt a party, then we shall receive 'respectful consideration.' We must be recognized as aggressive."[5]

We are far too well-behaved. We know that well-behaved women seldom make history. Let's be like our foremothers, the mass of angry, militant feminists that make men once again fear the power of women. Let's change our national priorities from wars to rights. Let's demand our fair share of our state's riches. Let's tell the truth of our foremothers' fight to make the world better for us. Let's finish the business they began. With our male allies backing us, let's kick us some ass and make us some history!

[5] Matilda Joslyn Gage, "The Political Outlook, (Syracuse, NY) *National Citizen and Ballot Box*, October 1879.

Above: Matilda Joslyn Gage, a progressive advocate of human rights, women's rights and principal but lesser-known activist of the 19th century woman suffrage movement in the United States.

Below: Her home is now the site of the Matilda Joslyn Gage Foundation in Fayetteville, NY. Learn more about Gage and her contributions at http://www.matildajoslyngage.org

Photos courtesy of the Matilda Joslyn Gage Foundation

LAURA LUSK

1984

Fourth grade, mock elections
I am the oddball that votes for Mondale and Ferraro
As we line up to go, Mr. Gleason asks "Why?"
Because there's a woman on the ticket.
Because half the population is women and we aren't represented.
Bewildered, he whispers "Feminist?!"

"We March for Choices": Girls at the January 21, 2017 Women's March.

Photo credit: Bethany Mackey

LIZ THOMPSON
A Woman's Life A Woman's Voice A Woman's Vote

It has been one hundred years since women in New York got the right to vote, to have a voice in civic and national affairs. That right changed the lives of many, but despite having made incredible strides since then, the reality is that women in New York, the United States and the world over are still the victims of various kinds of abuse as they continue on the journey toward social justice and equality.

Having the vote did not result in automatic respect for women, neither then nor now. As a short, fat, Black woman with natural hair, I encounter levels of discrimination, stereotyping and body shaming that are painful.

I saw a horrible example of this kind of hurtful disrespect and discrimination during the 2016 election campaign when the Director of the Clay County Development Corporation in West Virginia used her Facebook page to call First Lady, Michelle Obama, "an ape in high heels." Comments such as this, as well as some of the other rhetoric and behavior I witness, trouble me deeply. Sadly, I recognize that a tide in public conduct and discourse has turned, from a culture of tolerance to one of open intolerance.

The Facebook post made by the Clay County Director went viral, with those commenting either endorsing or decrying the vicious remark. At the time of this incident, I did not see the issue as one of free speech. In my view, it was about getting a person who served the public to understand that courtesy was necessary and was not mere political correctness, and that using racist, hate-filled rants and quips was not acceptable. At the time, this incident made me wonder how long it would take, in what I saw as a changing national climate, for people who privately hold racist views to start to publicly insulting those who were different. Would some of them refuse to provide services for Brown or Black people or others who were not White, or whom they regarded as unacceptably different?

I had no way of knowing then that I was soon to have my own "simian story," which would affect me so profoundly that it would take some weeks before I was able to share, talk or write about the experience in its entirety.

One afternoon I was standing in Penn Station, New York, next to a large, circular column. I was pretty much tucked out of the way behind this column because I was making a phone call and I wanted to complete it before going deeper into the subway and losing my connection.

While standing by the column, I saw a man walking in my direction with two "spinners" suitcases. I was not in his way so he fell off my radar. I continued with my call when, suddenly, I felt an intense pain on the toes of my right foot. I cannot say the man ran the suitcase over my foot deliberately, but he must have felt the bump the suitcase made when it left the floor and ran over my foot. The walker did not pause, stop, or say sorry, but continued rapidly on, leaving me in shock. I was not in his path and for his suitcase to reach my foot, the man and his suitcases had to veer off their walking line, move further to the right, avoid the column that was next to me, which he would have reached first, and still manage to run over my foot. In my view, that took a lot of "accidental steering."

I finished my business on the phone and went to catch the train for my meeting. There were empty seats on both sides of the train. I chose a block of three, sitting on the extreme right of the block, leaving two empty seats on my left. After a stop or two, a man got on the train. He chose not only to sit in the same block of seats I had chosen, but of the two empty seats next to me, he chose the one on my immediate left rather than the one on the extreme left.

Those of you who know the New York City subway culture know that if there are empty seats on the train, new passengers usually take the seat farthest away and not the one next to an already seated passenger. The practice generally is that new passengers only sit next to other people when the train is full and they have no other options.

Before the train could get to its next stop, the man who was now seated on my left started to talk loudly. He was being very obnoxious, but I ignored him. Then he leaned over and very deliberately said to me, "Look at you. Jesus Christ was a White man, but you are a fucking monkey!"

I did not respond or react. I kept my face devoid of expression. I said nothing. The man repeated his comment, laughing and becoming more crude and abusive. I did not turn. I did not look at him. My toes were still hurting from the suitcase being dragged over them. I sat with my eyes ahead. I said nothing. I never glanced in his direction.

I was actually praying, "Lord, this man is talking with his mouth, which he is entitled to do, but please do not let this man touch me!"

Other passengers looked on with sympathy, shock, disdain, disgust, amusement or anticipation. Their facial expressions suggested apparent support for the man, or support for me, but to the person, the passengers were silent. And my abuser did not stop his invective. Perhaps he hoped to goad or provoke me in some way and the fact that I would not speak, or even glance in his direction, shocked or annoyed him. Mine was probably not the reaction he was expecting.

He laughed as he repeated his description of me over and over. At every station, people got on and off. The train was filling up. All the passengers in the car looked on, waiting to see what would happen next, but no one came near us. No one took the empty seat next to the foul-mouthed man and me. No-one even stood near us. No one extended to him a word of rebuke or reproach. Not, "Stop it!" Not, "Leave the woman alone!" Not, "Behave yourself!" Not, "This woman has not troubled you!" Not, "This is unacceptable!" No one offered me a word of comfort, or came to my defense.

When should we speak out or stand up for each other? When and how do we acknowledge the other person's right and freedom simply to "be" -- a voter, a citizen, an immigrant, a passenger? To live in peace without being the object of scorn, suspicion, abuse or discrimination?

Sitting on the train that day, I heard the abuse this man directed at me. At times he turned fully toward me and I could smell his breath. Several scathing comments and putdowns occurred to me, but I did not let my mouth utter them. My mind went back to a day sixteen years ago, when someone tried to harm my father. I lost my temper, swore and behaved badly. Afterward, my Dad said to me, "Liz, always remember who you are."

In my mind's eye, I saw the face of my late father in front of me. I heard his voice in my ear. He was speaking quietly, gently, urging me to act with restraint. The sound of Dad's voice helped me to block out the voice and presence of the idiot on my left who was loudly calling me a monkey. I did nothing to escalate the situation. I could not help but think that since everyone remained silent while this man verbally abused me, they were unlikely to intervene if he became violent toward me. I prayed it would not come to that.

I sat on that train, silent. I remembered that I was raised to respect myself and others. I remembered what my parents and my country expected of me. I remembered that I was a professional with four academic degrees, and I thought, "Liz, you haven't done badly for a monkey." I smiled inwardly, but my outward expression did not change. I sat looking straight ahead without speaking. I remembered and took comfort in a statement made by First Lady Michelle Obama. After all the abuse to which she, President Obama, and their children were subjected, she was still able to say, "When they go low, we go high."

I remembered a wonderful quotation from George Bernard Shaw which I used in my recent motivational book, *Make Yourself Happy.* Shaw said, "Never wrestle with a pig, you both get dirty and the pig likes it." I determined that my abuser would not pull me down into the dirt and nastiness on the floor of the sty where he was clearly comfortable. I sat erect, legs crossed at the ankles, handbag on my lap, my face expressionless, mouth closed, eyes looking directly ahead.

Thankfully, I did not have far to go. In my head, I counted down the stops to my destination. Finally, we arrived at my stop. I remained seated until the last minute. Then, without giving the man time to react or follow, I headed quickly for the door and stepped onto the platform, away from my tormentor who was still on the train. The eye of every passenger followed me. I still had not uttered a word to the man or looked at him. Because I did not look at him during his tirade, to this day, I cannot identify the face of my persecutor. Nor can I identify the walker with the weaponized suitcases, who had moved away so rapidly after running over my toes that I did not get a glimpse at his face. These two men hurt me on the same day and I have no idea who they are, or what they look like.

A young White woman who also got off the train stopped on the platform and came across to speak to me. "I am so sorry," she said, apologizing for my abuser's behavior. She said that it was unacceptable. She was distressed at what she had witnessed. She said she didn't know how she would have reacted if anyone had treated her like that. She complimented me on how I had handled the situation. I thanked her for her kind words, knowing that she would never be called an ape or a monkey.

She was truly upset. She made a critical point, which was that she understood this was not an isolated incident. She said she could not imagine what it must be like having to face that kind of racism. I smiled. I knew that no one would ever see her dressed in a business suit in the first/business class lounge of an airline, assume she was a member of the wait staff and ask her to serve them their meal, as had happened to me.

I did not waste time asking her why she hadn't said a word to the man while we were on the train. Her heart was in the right place. Hopefully, she would encourage her friends, relatives, partners, colleagues and children, to take the high road and treat all members of the human family with courtesy, respect and dignity. Hopefully, she would maintain the view that we are all entitled to justice and equal opportunity. I thanked her again and bid her good evening.

She turned right. I went left. White and Black--each clothed in the skin given by God, skin that some individuals and societies use to define how White and Black and Brown people are treated in life and to some extent, their socioeconomic opportunity.

My foot and my heart were hurting. I took a deep breath and headed for my meeting. On the way, I wondered what other indignities were in store for me and for others who are different, as the bigots become more comfortable taking off their masks in the belief they have an ally in the White House.

I am in no doubt that this racist chose me because he saw an "easy" target--a short, middle-aged, overweight woman, alone. Yes, women in New York and the United States have the right to vote. Some of us no longer have to ride at the back of the bus, but being gracious, elegant, well-educated, well spoken, comporting ourselves with dignity and contributing positively to society, do not shield us from being body-shamed, abused, insulted, treated as unequal or second class, or from being discriminated against in relation to race, access to work, income or opportunity.

In the time since I have found my voice to speak out about this incident, I have encountered multiple and mixed reactions. Some people have expressed skepticism about the truth of it. At first this surprised me, but I have come to understand it is easier for them to call me a liar than to admit or confront the problem this incident reveals.

Others have expressed shock, outrage, disappointment or disbelief that no one intervened to stop my tormentor's tirade. Many have said that had they been present they would have remonstrated with my tormentor or shown their disapproval in some way. Perhaps, then again, perhaps not! Aren't we taught to avoid the "crazies" on the New York trains and not to get involved?

Other people have said the man had to be mentally ill. This too is an easy escape route which allows them to pretend that racism and its harmful consequences are not commonplace or widespread, just the product of a few mentally disturbed people. I have been asked whether my abuser was drunk, as if drunkenness should or would absolve him. When a drunk driver kills someone, does that make the death understandable, justifiable, excusable, acceptable, forgettable, inconsequential?

Some have asked why I said nothing or made no retaliatory remark. What were my options--to become as obnoxious and abusive as my persecutor, becoming the embodiment of the stereotypes of Black people that my abuser and others hold? If I had reacted would it have caused an escalation of my tormentor's behavior? Were there any limits to what he might have done? Would he have hurt me physically? Was he armed with a gun or carrying some other kind of weapon? If he had attacked me physically and I had been forced to defend myself, and the police were called, could I be sure that I would not have been harmed or shot? I have listened to people discuss this incident with the dispassion provided by the distance of time, place and personal circumstances. I lived the shock, fear and powerlessness of the experience.

The events of that day caused me much pain, but they also raised questions about continuing discrimination in the society. The issue now is, how do we ensure a just society in which we are all protected? A society in which those who are "different" are not subjected to discrimination, ridicule and abuse? I pray for grace, fortitude and protection in a changing American and international climate, which is becoming increasingly unfavorable to those who are "different."

One hundred years after the efforts of the suffragists in New York secured for women the right to vote, how should women now use their voices and their votes to protect each other and the space we have managed to carve out for ourselves? Most of all, for the sake of the next generation, how do we ensure that we keep moving forward and upward until gender discrimination is a no longer a reality, but a glimpse from our story, her story, his story, history?

My Dad said to me, "Liz, remember who you are." Perhaps America needs to remember the struggles of its women, who are deserving of respect and are still fighting to be treated as full and equal citizens in "the home of the free."

CHRISTINE EDWARDS
Speaking Up

Over the years, I never felt connected to the women's suffrage movement. I never felt that I could identify with it. My parents always performed their civic duty by voting in local, state and national elections, but it ended there. Once in a while my dad would pipe up with his views, but there was no conversation. There were no lessons within my family to learn about political activism. We didn't talk about politics because it wasn't polite.

My activism and political voice have only come to fruition this past year, in 2016. I had voted before then, but I'm ashamed to say, it wasn't a priority. I didn't think my voice really mattered. How could anyone hear my voice, in the sea of voices, especially that of a young woman? Looking at my past, maybe I'm more connected than I thought. I know my privilege. I feel it, but what about my voice all those years? Would things have been different if I had been a male? What was it like for women in my family?

I visited my grandma looking for some perspective on the suffrage movement and her voting experience. I was certain this amazing woman would have some insight to share with me; she always does. Her parents and her brother immigrated to the United States in 1920. My grandma was born in 1928, and as a first-generation citizen, was the first woman to vote in her family in 1946. She didn't recall any notable stories about voting or the movement, but she did have stories about what her life was like growing up. She said her father was very strict with her, but lenient with her brother. She was treated differently. There was a way things were done and you didn't question it, especially if you were a female.

I, too, was taught to be quiet. The treatment of females was ingrained in me—it was the way the world worked, society worked, religion worked. These teachings that molded me weren't outright oppression, but they were oppressive nonetheless.

At a very young age, my grandma lived through the Great Depression, World War II, and the loss of her mother and her brother. She gets very somber when talking about those days and she recalls how hard they were. I don't know exactly what I went looking for when talking with her that day, but I came away with the lesson of perseverance. I feel the weight of this lesson she gave me as the oldest of six grandchildren and as a woman. It is profound and timeless.

Over the years, women have persevered through so much. There are still many obstacles ahead of us today and battles that must be won, but I am certain that we can overcome them. I think of all of the women who fought for my right to speak up and the right to vote. My deepest gratitude goes to all of them, especially my grandma, who helped connect me with the past and taught me the lesson of perseverance, and of speaking up. I will speak my truth from my heart and I will vote. I will fight injustice, I will fight for equality, and I will fight alongside women to maintain the rights that my grandma helped us gain.

You will not be forgotten. To all of those women that came before me, I thank you. I've found my voice and I will never be silenced again.

Marching for American Womens' rights, then and now:

Above: Pre-election parade for suffrage in NYC, Oct. 23, 1915, in which 20,000 women marched.
Photo courtesy of Library of Congress, LC-USZ62-50393

Below: January 21, 2017 Women's March, a worldwide protest that is touted as likely the largest single-day demonstration in recorded United States history.
Photo by Alison Fromme

LISA HARRIS
Seneca Falls 1848-2017

Declaring sentiments is not the same as being sentimental,
Elizabeth Cady Stanton and Lucretia Mott knew.
Frederick Douglass chimed in as well, a freed black man who
    lived through hell.
All three declared to a group of 300, 18 grievances listed as a
    blueprint;
100 people signed it. Start women thinking and men will think,
    too.
Raise real questions, accept bad press, because all attention aids in
    the quest.
We all have a right to think and be heard,
denying all women and black men this right was absurd.

Speed ahead to 2017 and sort through the rhetoric
that now demeans women and black people,
Mexicans and Muslims, intellectuals and refugees,
immigrants and all of us who expect civil discourse,
logic and wisdom. The electoral college ignored,
once again, votes cast in favor by women and men.
The world watches us with horror and greed.

Amid allegations that voter fraud exists,
insistence that other lies and absurdities are true,
we find ourselves trapped in alternative facts and spinning crises.
President Trump plays a game of intimidation and uses
broken sentences to assert his successes, is willfully specious
and spurious with his claims. Refuse to lose your confidence.
Reclaim your full franchise as a citizen. Declare true sentiments

of justice, and refuse to yield to lies. The most recent rally
at Seneca Falls brought 10,000 people to question,
"What happened in this election? What is justice and when is it
    served?"
We are among those who decry tantrum behavior and alternative
    lies.
We seek peace and justice, once again, prefer the pen over the
    sword.

NORA SNYDER and ABBY GEORGIA SNYDER
Sylvia and Marsha P.

There is an urgency and pressure to SHOW UP, ACT, RESIST in our current social and political landscape. I think for many of us, choosing our own paths towards responsiveness, social responsibility, and political action is fraught with questions that never before felt so immediate and personal. We struggle with not only integrating our perspectives, experiences, and opinions, but also leveraging our time, talents, and strengths. None of this is new territory. However, there are times in history when a true accounting needs to take place, when we are forced to really face what is happening in the larger world and decide how we will proceed as individuals.

As a woman, I believe this can be an even more demanding task as we wrestle with daunting levels of emotional labor, societally reinforced self-doubt about strength and adequacy, and self-imposed guilt and false standards regarding being and doing enough. This energy is toxic--to ourselves and our endeavors. It debilitates and divides women and dilutes our social justice action just as our failure to be inclusive or intersectional did in the past.

Social media has become a new arena to make comparisons, not only regarding relationships and lifestyle, but now in addition to the daily onslaught of bad news reports. We are also inundated with images of all the stuff we are not doing and the relative privilege that we take for granted. In this swirl of shame and competition, we never quite get to the heart of the matter: how to harness our relative privilege to lift others.

Momentum cannot be built on shame. Once we start operating on obligation rather than pure motivation, and parsing out whose efforts matter and whose don't, who is sacrificing enough and who is not, we come dangerously close to determining who has value as a person.

I advocate bringing in a new chapter--a spirit of trust. Trusting ourselves to engage in a diversity of efforts, fueled by passion and commitment as we each take on what feels most relevant and right for each of us personally. And trusting women in general--with their bodies and their minds, their reproductive decisions, and whether or not they choose to wear a pussy hat.

The inspiration for my own contribution came packaged in a query from my millennial daughter. She asked me in her intense, serious way, "Did you know the Stonewall Riots were led by two WOMEN?"

In fact, I didn't. Much like my knowledge of the women's suffrage movement, my understanding of this event is full of gaps and misattributions. The Stonewall Riots were never emphasized in any school text or discussed in any classroom that I experienced, and my exposure to the history of the women's movement was only slightly less ignored. I remembered that President Obama declared the area around the Stonewall Inn as the first national monument to LGBT rights. I know I made the automatic assumption that white men must have been the leaders. Luckily, my daughter offered me her essay from her Women and Gender Studies class at Tompkins Cortland Community College to get me up to speed. I offer excerpts from her paper here, to tell this story that needs telling:

The Unsung Women Leaders of the Stonewall Riots by Abby Snyder
"In 1969, the Stonewall Inn was one of the few running Lesbian Gay Bi Trans (or LGBT)- centric bars. On June 28th, the New York City police initiated a raid on the bar attracting a crowd of over 150 civilians as the police wrongfully handcuffed and arrested groups of LGBT individuals. This happened often,

with constant raids on LGBT bars and hangouts, police focusing specifically on arresting LGBT individuals for even the smallest misdemeanor…

"However, this time the patrons of the bar (as well as the civilians drawn to the raid) fought back—tired and fed up with the constant police raids, brutalities, and injustices that LGBT people had endured for years….

"News of this riot spread quickly, and by the next night thousands of protestors rallied around the Stonewall Inn and fought the police that came to arrest them. This also happened a third night; and these riots are heralded as the beginning of the modern LGBT movement. These protestors consisted of LGBT people and non-LGBT people who supported and fought for LGBT rights…

"However, historical documentation of this movement did not give proper justice to the two pioneers of the initial riot at Stonewall. These two transgender women of color; Marsha P. Johnson and Sylvia Rivera, are the two leading (yet largely unrecognized) faces of the June 28th, 1969 Stonewall Inn riot…

"Marsha P. Johnson (1945-1992), a black transgender woman…became a strong activist for LGBT rights, probably due to the discrimination and transphobia she faced daily just for existing as a trans woman in society…

"Marsha also was an activist during the 1980s AIDS epidemic. She was seen doing demonstrations on Wall Street to protest the inordinate prices of experimental AIDS drugs. She also teamed up with activist Sylvia Rivera and founded the Street Transvestite Action Revolutionaries (S.T.A.R.), which was an activist group for transgender individuals…

"Marsha Johnson died in 1992. She was found in the Hudson River, having died under mysterious circumstances…. There have been attempts to reopen her case, however it is still currently closed.

"On the night of the Stonewall riot, Sylvia Rivera (1951–2002), a 17-year-old Puerto Rican drag queen (she would later come out as a trans woman),… is quoted as shouting, "I'm not missing a minute of this! It's the revolution!" Sylvia Rivera joined the Gay Activists Alliance (GAA) and became a very energetic and dedicated activist for LGBT rights and liberation. In particular, she campaigned for New York City to pass a Gay Rights Bill. She was famous for her arrest while climbing the walls of city hall in a dress and heels to crash a closed-door meeting discussing the bill.…

"Sylvia's work is being furthered by the continued work of SRLP (the Sylvia Rivera Law Project), an organization working towards ending poverty and discrimination regarding gender identity.…"

I am so grateful for this gift from my daughter, to add this story to my heart, to share it with others. I am glad to unveil my own ignorance of these events and often my consciousness is touched with details like poor Marsha P's broken body left like flotsam in the Hudson or the tragic mere thirty-five-year lifespan for trans women of color. Mostly I am in awe of their courage and commitment during such turbulent and hostile times. And this is where I detect an intersection between the "Unsung Heroes of the Stonewall Riots" and the suffragists: how they were willing to take a stand for themselves and others despite their obvious vulnerability. They shared the same steely determination in their eyes, ready to brave the bias, the inequities, the violence, the rape, the torture, the imprisonment, the humiliation, and the sheer hate at the hands of the powers that be, the law enforcement that was sworn to protect them, and their fellow citizens.

In the past, the women's suffrage movement made the grave error of getting ensnared in prejudices and fanning the flames of division, silencing some voices in order for others to be heard, seeking advantage through unfair play. All these transgressions—while remaining blind to the far greater power of unity over division! I can't even imagine the sheer magnitude such a movement would have—if all those seeking justice, opposing hate, and demanding equality stood together as one.

Am I being unkind to the suffragists? Too critical? I don't think so. Mostly because these women do not need my protection. These women were tough. They were dogged. They upended generations of social conditioning. They endured brutal forced feeding on filthy jailhouse floors. I firmly believe that if the suffragists were sitting with me today as I write this, they would not be asking for glorification. They would be sitting forward in their seats, rubbing their hands together, asking "What's next? How do we proceed? How do we utilize what we learned from the past for a better future?" These women, like Sylvia and Marsha P, were revolutionaries. They weren't satisfied with change being "possible," for them change is inevitable. Change is now. They aren't the ones who are going to be flinching at the past. Earlier I stated that "momentum cannot be built on shame." However, there are many attributes that *can* build momentum, like *truth*, like *humility*.

Imagine if Sylvia and Marsha P were welcomed into the fold and celebrated.

Imagine if we could work together to hold the line for human decency.

Imagine if we could all find our own ways of climbing the walls of city hall in a dress and heels.

Sylvia Rivera (holding the banner) and Marsha P. Johnson (with cooler) of the Street Transvestite Action Revolutionaries (S.T.A.R.) at the Christopher Street Liberation Day, Gay Pride Parade, NYC (24 June 1973). Photographer Leonard Fink. Reprinted, by permission, from National History Archives of the Lesbian, Gay, Bisexual & Transgender Community Center.

Marsha P. Johnson (with cooler) and Sylvia Rivera (holding banner) in New York City's Gay Pride March, 24 June 1973.
Photo by Leonard Fink, courtesy LGBT Community Center National History Archive.

STACEY MURPHY
Juanita Revisited

> *Suffrage has fallen, but it has fallen forward.*
> -- Juanita Breckinridge Bates, Chair of the Suffrage Party
> of Tompkins County, after a failed 1915 vote
> to pass the Suffrage Act

There is a fear of falling
That keeps me careful
Too full of care
To linger on the cliff's edge
To stick my turtle head out any farther
To venture onto the tightrope
To laugh too loud or dance too joyfully

Were my foremothers, bruised knees and scraped knuckles
Afraid?
Or did their thoughts stay with their daughters
Growls in their throats growing
As they wiped
The spit from men off their foreheads and
Persisted?

The time is gone for the luxury of my small fears.

What if from now on falling were flying
And landing face down on the mat
In a ring full of jeers
Mattered so much less
Than getting back up again?

Would we teach our daughters to pirouette
On the edges of ledges,
Shouting out math facts all the while,
Not waiting to be called on

Would they only think to love and not fear
Mid-flight breezes caressing their outstretched arms

And where would that finally get all of us, together,
If with every stumble, stagger, or tumble
We make sure we are falling only ever
Forward

THANK YOU JUANITA

AND ALL YOUR SISTERS IN THE SUFFRAGETTE MOVEMENT

During the 2016 election, Ithaca-area voters left their "I Voted" stickers and other mementos at the Ithaca grave of Juanita Breckinridge-Bates, chair of the Tompkins County Suffrage Party.

"We were all so gleeful, certain that we had just cast our votes for the first female president". –

Photo credit: Janelle Alvstad-Mattson, organizer of the effort

February 28, 2017 – This group of Democratic women wore suffragist white to President Trump's first Joint Address to Congress to show their unity in fighting any attempt to roll back progress for women during his Presidency.

Photo credit: Office of Congresswoman Chellie Pingree.

ABOUT THE WRITERS

Erica S. Brath is a journalist, writer, editor and artist currently living in Ithaca, New York. She has written for publications including *The Philadelphia Inquirer, Philadelphia Weekly* and *The Syracuse New Times,* and is a contributor to the book *Looking for Lockerbie.* She is currently working on a memoir about her experience living in a travel trailer full-time. Her website is esbrath.com.

Jennifer Cremerius is a marketing professional with a background in writing, editing, and journalism. She earned her MA in Writing and Publishing from DePaul University and her BA in English from the University of Illinois at Chicago. She now lives in upstate New York with her husband and two cats.

Nancy Avery Dafoe has published three books on teaching writing: *Breaking Open the Box; Writing Creatively;* and *The Misdirection of Education Policy* from Rowman & Littlefield in 2013, 2014, and 2016 respectively. Dafoe's hybrid memoir *An Iceberg in Paradise: A Passage through Alzheimer's* was published by SUNY Press. Her poetry chapbook *Poets Diving in the Night* was published by Finishing Line Press in January 2017. She won the 2016 Faulkner/Wisdom award in poetry.

Freeville native **Rachel Dickinson's work has appeared in numerous publications including *The Atlantic, Audubon,* and *Smithsonian.* Her latest book, released in 2017, is *The Notorious Reno Gang: the Wild Story of the West's First Brotherhood of Thieves, Assassins, and Train Robbers.* She has also authored several nonfiction books for middle-school aged children. Learn more about her at http://www.racheldickinson.com

Christine Edwards lives in Lansing, NY. She spends her time writing, having fun with her two boys, gardening and swimming in the lake. Her poetry appeared in the Spring 2017 edition of *States of Mind* magazine.

Yvonne Fisher is a psychotherapist, writer, artist, performer, and political activist. She has been a feminist for almost 50 years. Yvonne has written a series of stories, *My Jewish Mother*, which she has performed both locally and regionally over the last few years. She is engaged in the Resistance in pursuit of peace and justice.

Lisa Harris's novels make up *The Quest Trilogy: Geechee Girls* (winner of The Author Zone prize), *Allegheny Dream*, and *The Raven's Tale*, all published by the Ravenna Press. Her poetry book, *Traveling Through Glass*, with art work by Patricia Brown, is forthcoming in the spring of 2018 from Cayuga Lake Books. Her short stories and poems have been published in numerous journals. She lives in the Finger Lakes region of New York.

Sarah Jefferis is an author, editor, and writing consultant based in Ithaca, New York. Her writing consultant business is called: Write.Now. She works as a writing coach at the Office of Academic Diversity Initiatives at Cornell University. Her poetry books include *What Enters the Mouth* and *Forgetting the Salt*. Her nonfiction and poems have been published in *Rhino, The Mississippi Review, Stone Canoe, The American Literary Review* and other journals.

Deborah Jones is a woodworker who grew up in the Finger
Lakes and renovated her family barn into a home and studio. She
wrote a graphic novel, *The Barn Story*, about the building
experience. She has taught at Tompkins Cortland Community
College; the Women's Studies Program, Cornell University;
Center for Interdisciplinary Studies, Ithaca College; and at Wells
College, Aurora, N.Y. Her artwork has been included in local and
regional exhibitions. She is one the founders of The Greater
Ithaca Art Trail.

Carol Kammen has been the Tompkins County Historian since
2000. She is the author of numerous publications including *On
Doing Local History* (3 editions), *Zen and the Art of Local History*,
Glorious to View, *Part and Apart: the Black Experience at Cornell
1865-1945*, and *First Person Cornell*, and introductions for
numerous books including *From the Finger Lakes*. Carol has
written essays for *The Ithaca Journal* from 1978 to the present,
and local dramas including *Between the Lines*, *Counting Wheat Street*
and *Peaches & Bird*. She has also taught at Ithaca High School,
TC3, and Cornell University.

Marguerite Kearns is the granddaughter of Edna Buckman
Kearns (1882-1934), a New York State suffrage activist known for
her "Spirit of 1776" suffrage campaign wagon, now in the
collection of the New York State Museum in Albany. This
selection is from a work in progress, *Suffrage Wagon: A Memoir*
about years the author spent finding out about her grandmother
as told through stories shared by her grandfather Wilmer, mother
Wilma, and her own experiences growing up as a suffrage
descendant.

Laura Lusk is a homeschooling mother of two creative kiddos, and a librarian. She lives in the Finger Lakes region with her family.

Katharyn Howd Machan, author of 33 published poetry collections, Professor of Writing at Ithaca College, and former director of the national Feminist Women's Writing Workshops, Inc. lives in Central New York State. In 2012, she edited *Adrienne Rich: A Tribute Anthology* (Split Oak Press).

Buffalo native **Barbara Mink** has been an active painter since 1998, exhibiting often: http://barbaramink.com. Since 1986, Mink has been teaching MBA students in Cornell University's Johnson Graduate School of Management, specializing in oral and written communication. In 1989, she was elected to the Tompkins County Legislature and served for 12 years, five of them as Chair. In 2002 she founded a festival of art and science, the Light in Winter festival, and served as its Artistic and Executive Director until 2011.

Stacey Murphy lives in Ithaca, NY with her family. Her poems appear in the 2016 anthology *Wild Voices,* and in a number of online journals including the *Painted Parrot* and *Hedgerow.* She is a consultant to nonprofits and municipalities through her business, Murphy Grant Consulting.

Lynn Olcott is a retired teacher living in Cortland, New York.

Sally Roesch Wagner is Founder/Director of The Matilda Joslyn Gage Foundation in Fayetteville, N.Y. Adjunct faculty in The Renée Crown University Honors Program at Syracuse University and the St. John Fisher Executive Leadership

Program, Dr. Wagner is also a Public Scholar with Humanities New York.

Yael Saar was born and raised in Israel, and moved to NYC to go to college at the School of Visual Arts. A postpartum depression survivor, she is the founder of Mama's Comfort Camp peer support network, and teaches self kindness skills to dissolve anxiety, guilt, and shame, and increase creativity, clarity, and courage. She lives in Ithaca, N.Y., with her husband and two boys.

Nora Snyder writes for her website, http://www.illuminousflux.com. Her essays were published in the 2015 *Penned Parenthood Literary Magazine* and displayed at the 2015 Ithaca Festival's Social Justice Tent. Her work was featured as part of the 2016 World Goddess Day celebration. Nora's poetry is included in the 2017 *States Of Mind* literary magazine. She facilitates the writer support group, Writer's Block Party, the co-conspirator in this Anthology project.

Judy Swann is a poet, essayist, editor, translator, blogger, and bicycle commuter, whose work has been published in many venues both in print and online. Her book of letters, *We Are All Well: The Letters of Nora Hall*, appeared in 2014.

Liz Thompson is a writer, speaker, lawyer, consultant and contributor to the *Huffington Post*. She has spoken in more than forty countries, authored numerous articles and papers and co-authored two books on multilateralism and development. Her motivational book *Make Yourself Happy* was recently published. In 2008, she received the Champion of the Earth Award. Liz is also a former Assistant Secretary General of the United Nations. She was born in London, but served as a minister of government and senator in Barbados, which she regards as home. She divides her time between Barbados and New York. Liz holds LLM, MBA, LLB and LEC degrees.

Gaia Woolf-Nightingall is a British visual artist, writer and organic horticulturist, currently residing in the glorious surroundings of Ithaca NY.

ACKNOWLEDGEMENTS

The Tompkins County Proclamation declaring 2017 as the Year of the Woman in Tompkins County first appeared in the Tompkins County Legislature meeting on January 3, 2017.

"How to Reach an Understanding of One Aspect of Feminism," by Katharyn Howd Machan was written in the late 1970s and was first published in *Northeast Journal* 2, No. 2, October 1981 (Providence, R.I.).

"Let's Get Militant!" by Sally Roesch Wagner, PhD first appeared as a speech given at the Women's Suffrage Centennial Conference of the New York Cultural Heritage Tourism Network on October 7, 2016.

An earlier version of "A Woman's Life A Woman's Voice A Woman's Vote" by Liz Thompson appeared on the *Huffington Post* website as "Be Careful There Are Pigs on The Train in New York," February 6, 2017.

WITH THANKS

This Anthology project was informed and inspired by many people who contributed to its coming to be.

Thank you to the Community Arts Partnership of Tompkins County (CAP) for including this project in the Spring Writes Literary Festival, for the grant support for the initial printing of *NY Votes for Women: A Suffrage Centennial Anthology,* and for help in bringing the project to fruition.

Thank you to the History Center of Tompkins County for hosting us in its space for our readings, and for its enthusiastic aid in conceptualizing the project and connecting with others who are also commemorating the Centennial in Central New York.

Thank you to Edward Hower and the rest of the team at Cayuga Lake Books for helping us turn out the best collection we could, for your eagle-eyes in editing and experience and patience with this freshman effort at turning an idea into a book.

Thanks also to the Women's Rights National Historic Park and the National Women's Hall of Fame for taking such great care of our nation's history and artifacts, and for their ongoing efforts to keep Herstory available and accessible to women, men and especially children.

Special thanks go to Zee Zahava, writing teacher and mentor extraordinaire and 2017 Poet Laureate of Tompkins County, for many years of encouragement to several of the writers in this collection, and for her enthusiastic support of this project.

Thanks also to Jana Crawford for dusting off her editing and proofreading skills, and for always being interested in examining women's lives and issues, and of course for being supportive of her daughter.

Thank you to all the writers who contributed, and Jodie Mangor and Liz Burns who shared the anecdotes we mention in the introduction, and to others who have told us thought-provoking stories along the way.

Thank you to everyone who sent in pictures from the 2017 Women's Marches. We couldn't use all of them, but they all warmed our hearts. Thank you for taking part in history that day in January.

Finally, we want to thank the many kick-ass women in American history – the suffragists, the feminists in all waves, the Rosie the Riveters, the bra-burners, the ERA advocates, the women's libbers, the 2017 Women's Marchers, the scientists, those who fight in the halls of justice and Congress to protect women's rights, the writers, the doctors, the mothers, the aunties--all of us, together. Among these we are thankful to Juanita Breckenridge-Bates for reminding us all the way from 1915 of the importance of patience and perseverance in all things.

May all of us, if we fall, only ever fall forward.

CPSIA information can be obtained
at www.ICGtesting.com
Printed in the USA
LVOW03s1003271117
557718LV00002B/226/P